Colonial Law in America

Crime and Punishment

Robert M. Reed

4880 Lower Valley Road, Atglen, Pennsylvania 19310

Schiffer Books are available at special discounts for bulk purchases for sales promotions or premiums. Special editions, including personalized covers, corporate imprints, and excerpts can be created in large quantities for special needs. For more information contact the publisher:

Published by Schiffer Publishing Ltd.
4880 Lower Valley Road
Atglen, PA 19310
Phone: (610) 593-1777; Fax: (610) 593-2002
E-mail: Info@schifferbooks.com

For the largest selection of fine reference books on this and related subjects,
please visit our website at: **www.schifferbooks.com**
We are always looking for people to write books on new and related subjects.
If you have an idea for a book please contact us at the above address.

This book may be purchased from the publisher.
Include $5.00 for shipping.
Please try your bookstore first.
You may write for a free catalog.

In Europe, Schiffer books are distributed by
Bushwood Books
6 Marksbury Ave.
Kew Gardens
Surrey TW9 4JF England
Phone: 44 (0) 20 8392 8585; Fax: 44 (0) 20 8392 9876
E-mail: info@bushwoodbooks.co.uk
Website: www.bushwoodbooks.co.uk

Other Schiffer Books by the Author:
Advertising Postcards, 0-7643-1237-5, $29.95
The United States Presidents Illustrated, 978-0-7643-3280-7, $24.99
Christmas Postcards, A Collector's Guide, 978-0-7643-2689-9, $29.95
Greetings from Indianapolis, 978-0-7643-2629-5, $24.95
Greeings from Ohio: Vintage Postcards 1900-1960s, 0-7643-1711-3, $16.95
Greetings from Cleveland, Ohio 1900-1960, 978-0-7643-3025-4, $29.99
Greetings from Columbus, 978-0-7643-2885-5, $24.95
Greetings from Pittsburgh, 0-7643-2599-X, $24.95

Other Schiffer Books on Related Subjects:
Colonial Architecture: Early Examples from the First State, 0-7643-2510-8, $29.95

Copyright © 2011 by Robert M. Reed
Vintage postcards property of the author; images taken by Schiffer Publishing, Ltd.
Library of Congress Control Number: 2011924495

Designed by Mark David Bowyer
Type set in Adobe Caslon Pro / Humanist521 BT

ISBN: 978-0-7643-3780-2
Printed in the United States of America

Contents

Dedication 4
Acknowledgments.. 5
Introduction 6

Adultery.. 9
Babbling Women 13
Blasphemy 15
Burglary 20
Cursing 23
Debtors 25
Drunkenness 29
Guns to Church... 34
Horse Stealing 38
Idleness... 41
Indians 43
Liars 55
Punishment... 57
Rogues 63
Sabbath Breakers... 65
Schooling 71
Scolding 78
Slavery 80
Spinning and Weaving.................................. 94
Stealing 96
Taverns 98
Thanksgiving 101
Tobacco 103
Voting 106
Witchcraft... 108
Other Crimes and Laws 113
Historic Sites 120

Bibliography 128

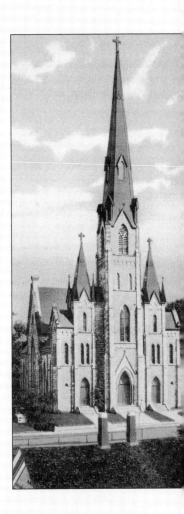

Dedication

This book on America's past is dedicated to Nicholas Orman Weger
and his generation that is America's future.

Acknowledgments

y sincere appreciation to Heather Reed, managing editor of *Antique and Collectible News Service*, who had contributed extensively to the editing and completion of this volume.

My highest regard here for the tireless contribution of John Brown Dillon, attorney and author of the work, *Oddities of Colonial Legislation*. Dillon's long enduring research in the nineteenth century recovered and restored vast amounts of Colonial law. He died in January of 1879 shortly before the huge volume was put into print.

A special bow here also to Rachel Faye Weger for gathering and confirming information regarding many Colonial-related historical sites around the United States. Thanks also to the many professional and volunteer staffs of these historical sites.

Introduction

The formation of this book on Colonial law began about thirty years ago, when a small regional museum decided to discard the entire contents of a tiny room of old law books.

Leather-bound and musty, the scores of once distinguished volumes of statues had all been published during the historic nineteenth century. It is likely that they had once adorned the shelves of a prominent firm practicing law within a decade or two of the Civil War.

Once I had hauled the carload of them home, I realized more than a few dealt exclusively with Colonial law. Of particular note was the remarkable *Oddities of Colonial Legislation* by John Dillon. His 784-page tome was printed during the 1870s shortly after his death.

Years of further reading and research revealed that as fascinating as Colonial laws were, a vast number had not been preserved over the centuries. Some have not been published since they appeared in those old law books of the nineteenth century. Thus it made this project more urgent and meaningful.

Government in the early Colonial days of America was generally one of absolute authority and power. Further that authority and power was regarded as being divinely guided and therefore unquestioned.

Generally the Colonists could establish their own laws and rules, but they fell heavily under the influence of the English power of King Charles I — at least in the New England Colonies.

In Old World terms, the people arriving at the Colonies were diverse. They brought various skills and trades. They represented various social and economic levels from indentured servants to wealthy landowners. Even their religious faiths were varied. But they were also subject to very determined leadership.

When it came to making laws they were zealots.

Chieftains sought to administer and mandate through their courts everything from gossiping to the theft of a loaf of bread. Punishment for what they considered to be criminal offenses was stern. Hundreds of different crimes called for the death penalty.

From adultery and babbling women to voting and witchcraft, many of the memorable ones have been gleaned from history, dusted off, and are presented here to remind us where we came from and how far we've come.

LANDING OF THE PILGRIMS. 1620. PLYMOUTH. MASS.　90963

Landing of the Pilgrims in 1620, Plymouth, Massachusetts.

Gate Entrance to Gardens of Royal Governor's Palace,
Williamsburg, Va.

9

Governor's Palace Gate, Williamsburg, Virginia.

Adultery

One of America's most enduring novels, *The Scarlet Letter*, was written as fiction by Nathaniel Hawthorne, but the laws it detailed were factual. In the novel a young woman is forced to wear a scarlet letter "A" on her clothing as punishment for the crime of adultery. Obviously she was subjected to the scorn and ridicule of the community.

In the true world of Colonial law, her exact punishment could have, and likely would have, been much worse. In 1673 Connecticut, the punishment for the crime of adultery by a married woman — as was the status of the fictional Hester Prynne — called for whipping the naked body of the offender while the offender was tied at the stake. Further, it offered the additional option of the use of a "hot iron" to indeed brand the letter "A" upon the forehead of the evildoer. Any of the above also included the usual wearing of the scarlet letter in a prominent place on the clothing as well.

In those days of early America, it was held that any such "heinous transgressions" be dealt with severely. Perhaps the offenders would escape the death penalty, but they would be clearly marked...to be mocked by all who happened to pass by them.

Even two unmarried persons could be judged guilty of the crime of adultery. However, the laws were usually much more harsh if one or both of the parties were actually married.

Other cultures in other times may have handled such offending relations less severely or even more discreetly than a scarlet letter or a public flogging. It was not so however in the Colonial world. It was a time and place where, as one Massachusetts woman proclaimed, "The air of the country is sharp, the rocks many, the trees innumerable, the grass little, the winter cold."

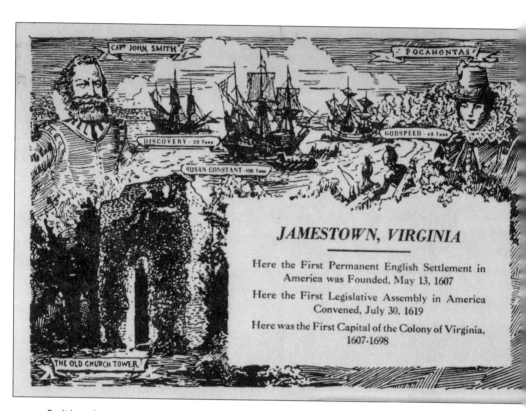

CAPT. JOHN SMITH

POCAHONTAS

DISCOVERY · 20 Tons

GODSPEED · 40 Tons

SUSAN CONSTANT · 100 Tons

THE OLD CHURCH TOWER

JAMESTOWN, VIRGINIA

Here the First Permanent English Settlement in
America was Founded, May 13, 1607

Here the First Legislative Assembly in America
Convened, July 30, 1619

Here was the First Capital of the Colony of Virginia,
1607-1698

English settlement in 1607, Jamestown, Virginia.

Connecticut, 1673

"It is ordered by this court and the authority thereof, that whomever shall commit adultery with a married woman, or one betrothed to another man, both of them shall be severely punished by whipping on the naked body, and stigmatized or burnt on the forehead with the letter A on a hot iron, and he or she shall wear a halter about his or her neck on the outside of their garments during his or her abode in this colony, so as it may be visible; and as often as he or she shall be found without their halter, worn as aforesaid, they shall, upon information and proof of the same, made before any assistant or commissioner, be by them ordered to be whipped."

New Hampshire, 1680

"It is enacted by this Assembly that whosoever shall commit Adultery with a married woman; or one betrothed to another man, both of them shall be severely punished by whipping (the) two several times, not exceeding 40 lashes, once when ye Court is sitting at which they were convicted of the fact, and the second time as the court shall order.

"Likewise shall wear two capital letter A.D. cut out in cloth and sowed on their uppermost garments on their arms or back, and if at any time they shall be found without the said letters so worn white in this Government, to be forthwith taken and publicly whipped, and so from time to time as often as they are found not to wear them."

New Jersey, 1694

"Whereas, amongst other heinous transgressions for which God Almighty afflicts a land, the sin of uncleanness is one of the greatest in the eyes of a pure God, for the suppression and discouragement of which, be it enacted by the governor, council and representatives in this present Assembly and assembled, and by the authority of the same, that what person so ever, man or woman, shall be convicted thereof before any court of record, either by confession of the party, or other evident proofs, such person or persons so convicted (if both parties are unmarried) shall be fined in the some of five pounds.

"And if either party is married, in the sum of ten pounds, together with the costs of court.

"And in case of non-payment of the fine to be imposed as foresaid, to receive at the most public place where the crime shall be adjudged, thirty-nine stripes on the bare back, if either party is married persons, and if both married, then twenty stripes on the bare back, as aforesaid, unless they petition to be sold to serve a certain space of time, at the discretion of the court, to pay the fine and court charges aforesaid; and that the said person so convicted, as above, shall be bound in a recognizance to our sovereign lord and lady, the king and queen's majesties, in the sum of fifty pounds for good behavior for the space of a year and a day thereafter."

Babbling Women

In the days of Colonial America women who seriously and openly disagreed with their husbands could be subject to prompt and harsh punishment.

The status of a woman in those days, while above that of a servant or a slave, was certainly not in any sense equal to that of a Colonial man. While most white women could attend some of the elementary schools, they were usually denied the privilege of attending the higher educating grammar schools. Records show, for example, that during the early part of the eighteenth century nearly two-fifths of the women living in Massachusetts could not write their own names.

Thus it is not surprising that there was written punishment for "babbling women." The law cited here is from Virginia in 1662, but other settlements used similar wording to administer similar punishment.

"Whereas, many babbling women slander and scandalize their neighbors, for which their poor husbands are often involved in chargeable and vexatious suits, and cost in great damages. Be it therefore enacted by the authority aforesaid, that in actions of slander, occasioned by the wife, after judgment passed for the damages the woman is punished by ducking.

"And if the slander be so enormous as to be judged at greater damages than five hundred pounds of tobacco, then the woman to suffer ducking for each five hundred pounds of tobacco adjudged against the husband, if he refuses to pay the tobacco."

Typically the judgment of deciding the woman's guilt was left to any local official. To a woman deemed to have been particularly nagging or quarrelsome the decree was for ducking. Most villages had a functioning ducking stool for punishing what were then considered relatively minor offenses.

The ducking stool itself was typically a wooden seat held by two beams of about twelve to fifteen feet. Once the offender was seated and tied, the beams could then be swung away from the bank of the pond or river and into the water.

There are also accounts of rare cases when both the wife and husband were bound back to back and given double ducking for good measure.

Kitchen in Governor's Palace, Williamsburg, Virginia.

Blasphemy

In the days of Colonial life in America, the act of blasphemy was defined as showing a lack of respect for God. In all the land it was a major crime. Blasphemy could be a deadly criminal act.

Throughout the colonies more than three hundred crimes could ultimately be punishable by death — blasphemy was sometimes one of them.

Consider the order from Sir Thomas Gates, Lieutenant General of Virginia in 1610. As quoted from the *Articles, Laws and Orders, Divine, Politique and Martial*, for the Colony in Virginia:

> "No man (shall) speak impiously or maliciously against the Holy and Blessed Trinity, or any of the Three Persons, that is to say, against God the Father, God the Son, and God they Holey Ghost, or against the known articles of the Christians faith, upon pain of death."

Lt. General Gates took it a little further by adding:

> "No man shall use any traitorous words against His Majesty's person, or royal authority, upon pain of death."

And finally:

> "No man shall speak any word, or do any act, which may tend to the derision or despite of God's Holy word, upon pain of death."

The general's stern directive was to order each man and woman in the colony to "give us an account of his and their faith and religion, and repair unto the minister, that by his conference with them he may understand and gather whether theretofore they have been sufficiently instructed in the principles and grounds of religion, whose weakness and ignorance herein the minister finding and advising them, in all love and charity, to repair often unto him, to receive therein a greater measure of knowledge."

French Catholic Church, St. Johnsbury, Vt.   54552-N

Catholic Church, St. Johnsbury, Vermont.

16

There were consequences for not abiding.

> "If they refuse so to repair unto him, and he, the minister, give notice thereof to the governor, or that chief officer of that town or fort, wherein he or she, the parties so offending, may remain, the governor shall cause the offender, for the first time of refusal, to be whipped."

Not paying proper attention to the minister after the first offense became considerably more serious in early 1600s Virginia. For the second refusal to counsel with the minister, they were to be "whipped twice, and to acknowledge his (or her) fault upon the Sabbath day in the assembly of the congregation." Further refusal could develop into punishment on a daily basis.

> "And for the third time to be whipped every day until he (or she) hath made the same acknowledgement and asked forgiveness for the same, and shall repair unto the minister to be further instructed aforesaid; and upon the Sabbath, when the minister shall catechize and demand any question concerning his faith and knowledge, he shall not refuse to make answer upon the same peril." *(See Sabbath Breakers chapter)*

The curse of blasphemy continued to be dealt with severely in the Colonies in somewhat creative ways. If whipping failed, there was always the gauntlet or a hot iron to the tongue. The pillory was sometimes offered as an alternative, and there was the branding of the letter "B" on the forehead.

A 1676 extract from the "articles, rules and orders to be observed and kept by the army as well in the several garrisons as in the field" prescribed the following for blasphemy:

> "If any shall blaspheme the name of God, either drunk or sober, shall for every offense run the gauntlet through 100 men or thereabouts, either more of less, at the discretion of the commander, but he or they that shall willfully, notoriously and obstinately persist in this wickedness shall be bored through the tongue with a hot iron.
>
> "If any person or persons in the army shall deride or contemn God's word or sacraments, they shall suffer and undergo the foresaid punishment."

Other laws in the Colonies offered the pillory as a punishment for blasphemy. Typically the pillory involved the offender sitting in chair-like device, which had a wooden frame with holes for holding the head and hands over an extended period. It was nearly always a source of public shame and humiliation. In some cases tormentors were free to hurl insults as well as fruits and vegetables at the pilloried offender.

Massachusetts, 1697

"Be it declared and enacted by the lieutenant-governor, council, and representatives convened in General Court or Assembly, and it is enacted by the authority of the same, that if any person shall presume willfully to blaspheme the holy name of God, Father, Son, or Holy Ghost, either by denying, cursing, or reproaching the true God, his creation, or government of the world; or by denying, cursing, or reproaching the Holy Word of God, that is, the canonical scriptures contained in the books of the Old and New Testament… Everyone so offending shall be punished by imprisonment not exceeding six months, and until they find sureties for the good behavior, by setting in the pillory, by whipping, boring through the tongue with a red-hot iron, or setting upon the gallows with a rope about their neck at the discretion of the Court of Assize and General Jail Delivery, before which the trail shall be, according to the circumstances, which may aggravate or alleviate the offense."

Pennsylvania, 1700

"An act to prevent the grievous sins of cursing and swearing within this province and territories: And be it further enacted, That whomever shall willfully, premeditatedly, and despitefully blaspheme or speak loosely and profanely of Almighty God, Christ Jesus, the Holy Spirit, or the Scriptures of Truth, and is legally convicted thereof, shall forfeit and pay the sum of ten pounds, for the use of the poor in the county where such offense shall be committed, or suffer three months imprisonment at hard labor as aforesaid, for the use of said poor."

Carolinas, 1703

(Author's Note: Carolina was not divided into North Carolina and South Carolina until 1721.)

"Whereas some persons have of late years openly avowed and published many blasphemous and infamous opinions, contrary to the doctrines and principles of the Christian religion, greatly tending to the dishonor of Almighty God, and may prove destructive to the peace and welfare of this province: We therefore, for the more effectual suppressing of the said detestable crimes, be it enacted that if any person, having been educated in, or at any time have made profession of the Christian religion within this province, shall, by writing, printing, teaching, or advised speaking, deny any one of the persons of the Holy

Trinity to be God, or shall assert or maintain there are more Gods than one, or shall deny the Christian religion to be true, or the Holy Scriptures of the Old and New Testament to be of divine authority, and, shall, upon indictment or information in any of the courts of record within this part of the province, be thereof lawfully convicted by the oath of two or more credible witnesses, such person or persons for the first offense shall be adjudged incapable and disabled in law, to all intents and purposes whatsoever, to have or enjoy any office or offices, be member of the Assembly, or have or enjoy any employments, ecclesiastical, civil or military, or any part in them.

"And if any persons or persons so convicted as aforesaid shall, at the time of his conviction, enjoy or possess any office, place of trust, or employment, such office, place of trust, or employment shall be void, and is hereby declared void."

A second conviction was punishable by the infliction of other penalties, and "imprisonment for the space of three years, without bail or mainprise, from the time of such conviction."

Delaware, 1741

"If any person shall willfully or premeditatedly be guilty of blasphemy, and shall thereof be legally convicted, the person so offended shall, for every such offense, be set in the pillory for the space of two hours, and be branded in his or her forehead with the letter B, and be publicly whipped, on his or her bare back, with thirty-nine lashes well laid on."

Connecticut, 1750

"Be it enacted by the governor, council and representatives in General Court assembled, and by the authority of the same, That if any person within this colony shall blaspheme the name of God, the Father, Son, or Holy Ghost, with direct, express, presumptuous and high-handed blasphemy, or shall curse in the like manner, such person shall be put to death."

Burglary

I t will probably come as no surprise that Colonial crimes such as burglary were usually very harshly dealt within the settlements.

A first offender might get off with a mere branding with a hot iron upon the right hand with the letter "B" or a public whipping. However the crime could involve the lopping off of the offender's ears, or at least having one ear nailed to a post.

Finally there was the death penalty.

Many modern day historians have suggested that most of the people committing theft-related crimes such as burglary were not hardened criminals, but were more likely to be simply those unable to locate gainful employment in the Colonies. Many Colonial laws were enacted to restrict a person's right to switch from one trade to another (See "Taverns").

"Such laws made it impossible for a skilled workman to get employment outside his own line," writes historian J. R. H. Moore in the book, Industrial History of the American People, "no matter how badly he might be in need of work."

Thus no matter what the provocation, the burglary or theft of even an item of relatively little value would likely bring severe if not deadly punishment.

"The result of such savage laws was the execution of many a destitute man who had taken to theft (or burglary) in desperation to provide food for his family," observed author Moore.

Slowly times changed.

During the course of the seventeenth and eighteenth centuries public opinion in governing England and in the Colonies to a lesser degree underwent a transition. "It became evident that the community was robbing itself (to pardon the pun) of many a valuable life by merciless execution of an unjust law that might once have valuable, but no longer needed."

Generally the population grew unhappy with the increasing cost of enforcing the so-called poor laws, which were widespread and numerous. Obviously the families of the poor were not pleased with such severe punishments.

CHRISTOPH AND JOHN VOGLER HOUSES, OLD SALEM

Christoph and John Vogler homes, Winston-Salem, North Carolina.

Colonists as a rule could not bring themselves to really repeal any law, however stern, which had been on the statue books for a long time. Instead they gradually moved toward a moderation of the punishment itself.

"So in order to show mercy to a man arrested for stealing, the prisoner was charged with having stolen property to the value of five shillings eleven pence," according to Moore, "then the judge could sentence him to transportation (a sort of work detail), and a strong man, who probably was not a criminal by instinct, was saved to perform for the country valuable service in the Colonies."

Dealing with such 'poor' crimes, though, did not begin in moderation.

Province of New Hampshire, 1679

"For as much as many persons of late years have been and are apt to be injurious to the Lives and Goods of others, notwithstanding all Laws and means to prevent the same, it is therefore ordered by this Assembly and ye authority there of if any person shall commit Burglary by breaking up any dwelling house or ware house, or shall forcibly rob any person in the field or highways, such offenders shall for the first offence be branded on the right hand with the letter B.

"And if he shall offend in the like kind a 2nd time he shall be branded on the other (hand) and be severely whipped.

"And if either was committed on the Lord's day his brand shall be set on his forehead, and if he shall fall into the like offense for the 3rd time he shall be put to death as being incorrigible, or otherwise grievously punished, as the court shall determine."

Connecticut, 1750

"Be it enacted by the governor, council and representatives in general court assembled, and by the authority of the same, that whosoever shall commit burglary by breaking up any dwelling house or shop wherein goods, wares and merchandises are kept, or shall rob any person in the field or highway, such person so offending shall, for the first offense, be branded on the forehead with the capital letter B, on a hot iron, and have one of his ears nailed to a post and cut off, and also be whipped on the naked body fifteen stripes.

"And for the second offense such person shall be branded, as aforesaid, and have his other ear nailed and cut off, as foresaid, and be whipped on the naked body twenty-five stripes; and if such person shall commit the offense a third time he shall be put to death as incorrigible."

Cursing

eople living in Colonial America had to watch their language. That is anything beyond darnth and dangth ye.

Like so many other "crimes" of that era, cursing and swearing was a punishable offense in settlements throughout the Colonies. To be sure, to be profane was not usually as serious an offense as, say, adultery or witchcraft, but it was nevertheless dealt with steadfastly.

Typically the act of cursing or swearing was punished in the Colonies with a fine for the first time. The second or third offense, however, was looked upon with more scorn. A serious potty mouth could expect to do time on the pillory or stocks, or even be jailed for an undefined period.

An exception to the overall attitude, however, involved cursing one's parents. Some early Colonial law, including New Hampshire, called for anyone above 16 years of age to be subject to the death penalty. The teenager was exempted in certain circumstances such as being subject to cruel treatment or if their life was indeed in peril, but in the late 1600s a foul-mouthed teenager could be in big trouble.

Virginia, 1676

"If any man shall offend God's name by swearing or notorious drunkenness, and shall be thereof thrice convicted by his officer, and shall still obstinately persist therein, he shall, after the third offense, and for every such offense afterwards, ride the wooden horse half an hour with musket tied to each foot, and ask forgiveness at the next meeting for prayer or preaching."

Province of New Hampshire, 1679

"If any child or children above 16 years old, of competent understanding, shall curse or smite their natural father or mother, he or they shall be put to death, unless it can be sufficiently testified that the parents have been unchristianly negligent of ye education of such children.

"Or so provoked them by extreme cruel correction that they have been forced thereunto to preserve themselves from death or maiming."

New Hampshire, 1701

"Cursing and swearing made punishable by fine of one shilling for the first offense, or be set in the stocks for two hours, if unable to pay fine.

"For every oath or curse after the first, two shillings, or be set in the stocks not exceeding three hours."

Powder magazine, Williamsburg, Virginia.

Debtors

In the early Colonial days debtors were usually imprisoned until their debts were paid in full.

It may be a reasonable question to wonder just how one's debts would be paid if the offending debtor were behind bars. There are a couple of answers. One might be that a friend, a relative, or an inheritance would pay the debt off; the latter, which was far more likely in Colonial America, might be a matter of serving several years, perhaps seven years, in prison. While the system consider debtors much more the 'victims of misfortune' that criminals, they were still often given prison time.

One type of indebtedness involved indentured servants.

The indentured servant business prevailed in the Colonies in part because there were so many people in England who were doing quite poorly and saw the New World as an opportunity to better themselves. Meanwhile, in the early days of the Colonies, all types of manpower was greatly needed.

The would-be servant or worker usually did not have the cash for a costly voyage from Europe to the American Colonies. A solution was a contract of servitude where the passenger would sign an agreement with the ship's captain. Under the general terms of the agreement the passenger would agree to about six or eight years of labor as a servant. Once the ship arrived in the Colonies the captain or his agents sold the agreement to whoever needed a servant and had the means to pay.

This agreement was called "indentured" because of the shape of the paper it was written on. The form was written in duplicate on a large sheet. The halves of the sheet were separated by a wavy or jagged cut called an indent. The common name of that class of that servant thus became an indentured servant.

Such indentured servants, while still clearly committed to labor, were far from the horror of slavery *(see "Slavery")*.

Indentured servants had rights that were protected by laws in the Colonies. Generally during the term of service the master was required to provide food, clothing, and shelter, and with other things which may be necessary. At the end of the required years of service the master was obliged by law to give his servant some clothing. It some cases a small amount of money and a musket were a part of the closing bargain.

Moreover, servants were allowed to own property, and in some cases a particularly industrious servant was able to buy the last part of his required service with any small amount of wealth that had been accumulated.

However, not all relationships with indentured servants and their masters went that well. Sometimes these servants ran away. In some regions, owners of the 'debt' were forced to advertise in newspapers describing the runaway and seeking their return. Usually the owner offered a small reward and perhaps any 'reasonable' expenses in returning the missing servant.

In other areas a serious punishment awaited the runaway indentured servant. This could include a doubling of the term of indentured service. In certain cases, a second offender might be branded in the cheek with a letter "R" and lose whatever rights the servant had once held. Oddly one Virginia law called for the master of runaways to "cut or cause to be cut the hair of all such runaways close above the ears." The haircut was, at the time, believed to make the runaway more likely to be discovered and apprehended in another runway was attempted.

Debtors Prison (gaol), Williamsburg, Virginia.

Massachusetts, 1641

Imprisoned For Debt

"Provided, nevertheless, that no man's person shall be kept in prison for debt, but when there is an appearance of some estate which he will not produce, to which end any court of commissioners, authorized by the general court, may administer an oath to the part of any other suspected to be privy in concealing his estate.

"But shall satisfy by service if the creditor require it, but shall not be sold to any but of the English nation."

Virginia, 1643

Runaway Servants

"Whereas, there are divers loitering runaways in the colony who very often absent themselves from their masters' service, and sometimes in two or three months can not be found, whereby their masters are at great charge in finding them, and many times even to the lost of their year's labor before they be had.

"Be it therefore enacted and confirmed, that all runaways that shall absent themselves from their said masters' service shall be liable to make satisfaction by service at the end of their time by indenture double the time of service so neglected, and in some cases more, if the commissioners for the place find it requisite and convenient.

"And if such runaways shall be found to transgress the second time, or oftener (if it shall be duly proved against them), that than they shall be branded in the cheek with the letter "R" and pass under the statue of incorrigible rogues: provided, notwithstanding, that where any servants shall have just cause of complaint against their masters or mistresses by harsh or unchristian like usage or other ways, for want of diet or convenient necessaries, that then it shall be lawful to make his or their complaint."

Virginia, 1659

Knowing Runaway Servants

"Whereas, the act for runaway servants appoint only the punishment of the said servants and the penalty of entertaining them, but provides not way for the discovery of them, it is enacted and ordained that the master of every such runaway shall cut or cause to be cut the hair of all such runaways close above the ears, whereby they may be with more ease discovered and apprehended."

Pennsylvania, 1705

Debtors Pay by Servitude

"No person shall be kept in prison for debts or fines longer than the second day of the next sessions after his or her commitment, unless the plaintiff shall make it appear that the person imprisoned hath some estate that he will not produce; in which case the court shall examine all persons suspected to be privy to the concealing of such estate.

"And if no estate sufficient shall be found the debtor shall make satisfaction by servitude, according to the judgment of the court were such action is tried (not exceeding seven years, if a single person and under the age of fifty and three years, or five years, if a married man and under the age of forty and six years), if the plaintiff require it. But if the plaintiff refuse such manner of satisfaction, according to the judgment of the court, as aforesaid, then, and in such a case, the prisoner shall be discharged in open court."

Drunkenness

In the early days of the American Colonies it would seem Colonists were obsessive about their drinking and compulsive about punishing its excessiveness.

Perhaps it was the hard life on the frontier or perhaps it was growing accustom to regularly imbibing during the daunting voyage across the ocean to the new land. Whatever the reason was that could have caused it, consumption of liquor was extensive in the Colonies.

One historian quipped that Colonial citizens in fact drank everything but water. A bit of an over statement perhaps, but nevertheless it bore a ring of truth.

It was well known, for example, that Roanoke Island settlers in the Virginia Colony were among the first to make ale. It was relatively easy to make even for those who had relative limited resources. Basically it just called for mashed corn (or maze) and water. Once combined time would enable the mixture to ferment and then it could be consumed.

Soon details of the process had spread and creative Colonists began to use other available grains such as barley and rye to make additional intoxicating brew. While the first American brewery was operational even before 1625, brewing was commonplace in Colonial homes long before that time.

For further variety the Colonies were abundant with both non-alcoholic cider and alcoholic 'hard' cider. Cider of both types was readily available to Colonial homes due in part to the fact that it could easily be gathered from the land and needed little processing.

And there was the ever present rum.

Rum comprised a major industry in the Colonies. Workers used imported molasses from the West Indies to make rum, which was a very popular drink throughout the Colonies. Other shipments of molasses were sent to Africa where they were used to trade for slaves. Often some of these particular slaves were then traded in the West Indies for more molasses.

At one time the wealthier classes in the Colonies enjoyed a very fashionable toddy, which included water, sugar, nutmeg, and a generous amount of rum. It was often a favorite at a Colonial lunch.

"At weddings, funerals, christenings, at all public meetings and private feasts, New England rum was ever present," noted Alice Morse Earle writing in the book, *Home Life In Colonial Days*.

About the only alcoholic drink not especially popular in the Colonies was wine. Though enterprising Colonists made wine in significant numbers, they generally chose to export it rather than consume it in large quantities.

Surprisingly in view of the rigid lifestyle and laws of early America, children were allowed to drink nearly every type of alcoholic beverage that adults could consume. The children might be given a serving that was watered-down or otherwise diluted, but was still hard liquor.

Simply put the drinking of booze was frequent and widespread in the Colonies, which led directly to the problem of chronic (and often public) drunkenness in these otherwise reserved communities.

Earle concluded in a book, *Colonial Life*, written in 1898: "In nothing is more contrast shown between our present day and colonial times than in the habits of liquor-drinking. We cannot be grateful enough for temperance reform, which began in the early part of this nineteenth century, and was so sadly needed."

Back in Colonial America even high-ranking politicians were not exempt from punishment for public drunkenness. Consider the case of an Assemblyman in 1666 Maryland.

In those times, only the very rich and powerful could be considered for such a position in the General Assembly. Usually qualifications included owning slaves, hundreds of acres of land, and other property considered to be of significant value. The Assemblyman is unnamed in this account, but his offense and punishment was specific.

According to one published account, the Assemblyman had "disturbed the whole house by calling them papists, rogues, pitiful rogues, puppies" and more. The Maryland Upper House ordered him to be brought fourth by the sheriff on charges of being rude and insulting.

The offending Assemblyman told the group that he remembered none of the words alleged, but he was indeed drunk. The Upper House adjudged the answer to be altogether unsatisfactory, "and no person of full age should take advantage of drunkenness in such a case."

It was the ruling of the Upper House that the offender be tied to an apple tree before the house of Assembly and whipped on the bare back for thirty-nine lashes. He was then to be "brought into both houses of Assembly, and made to ask their forgiveness."

New Jersey, 1668

That Beastly Vice

"Concerning that beastly vice drunkenness, it is hereby enacted, that if any person be found to be drunk he shall pay one shilling fine for the first time, two shillings for the second, and for the third time and for every time after two shillings and six pence.

"And such as have nothing to pay shall suffer corporal punishment; and for those that are unruly and disturbers of the peace they shall be put in the stocks until they are sober, or during the pleasure of the officer in chief of the place where he is drunk."

New Hampshire, 1679

Drunk At Any Time

"For as much as it is observed yet the sin of drunkenness doth greatly abound, to the dishonor of God, impoverishing of such as fall into it, and great of such as are sober minded, for prevention of ye growing.

"It is enacted by this assembly, and yet authority thereof, that, whatsoever person shall be found drunk at any in any Tavern, ordinary, alehouse, or elsewhere in this Province, and be legally convicted thereof, he or they shall for the first default be fined five shillings, and for the second default ten shillings; and if he or they will not or can not pay the fine, then to be set in the Stocks not exceeding two hours.

"And for the third transgression to be bound to yet good behavior; and if he shall transgress a fourth time, to pay five pounds and be publicly whipped, and so from time to time as often as they shall be found transgressors in that kind.

"By drunkenness it is to be understood one that lisps or falters in his speech by reason over much drink, or that staggers in his going, or that vomits by reason of excessive drinking, or that cannot by reason thereof follow his calling."

Massachusetts, 1693

Caging Drunkards

"Whereas, the breach of sundry criminal laws of this province is only punishable by fines, and many times the breakers of them have not money to satisfy the same; be it therefore enacted by the governor, council and representatives convened in General Assembly, and by the authority of the same, that henceforward it shall be in power of any justice of the peace that shall have cognizance thereof.

"To punish breakers of the peace, profaners of the Sabbath, and unlawful gamesters, drunkards, or profane swearers or cursers, by sitting in the stocks of putting into the cage not to exceed three hours, or imprisonment 24 hours, or by whipping, not exceeding ten stripes, as the case may deserve, and where the offender has not wherewithal to satisfy the law that the case provided."

Public Gaol, Williamsburg, Virginia

Pillory or stocks, Williamsburg, Virginia.

New York, 1708

Drunkenness in Slaves

"Every Negro, Indian, or other slaves that shall be found guilty of any of the above said facts (drunkenness, cursing, or swearing), or talk impudently to any Christian, shall suffer so many stripes, at some public place, as the justice of the peace in such place where such offense is committed shall think fit, not exceeding forty."

New Hampshire, 1719

Drunkards to be Posted

"And it be further enacted by the authority aforesaid, the selectmen in each town shall cause to be posted up in all public houses within each town in this province, a list of names of all persons reputed drunkards or common tipplers, misspending their time and estates in such houses.

"And every keeper of such house, after notice given him, as aforesaid, that shall be convicted before one or more justices of the peace of entertaining or suffering any of the persons named in such list to drink or tipple in his or her house, or any the dependencies thereof, shall forfeit and pay the sum of twenty shillings; one money thereof to him of them who shall inform of the same offense, and the other money to and for the use of the poor of the town were such offense shall be committed."

North Carolina, 1741

Drunkenness on the Lord's Day

"And it be further enacted by the authority aforesaid, that every person convicted of drunkenness, by view of any justice of the peace, confession of the party, or oath of one or more witness or witnesses, such person so convicted shall, if such offense was committed on the Lord's Day, forfeit and pay the sum of five shillings of the like money; but it on another day, the sum of two shillings and sixpence for each and every offense."

Guns to Church

ong before the Second Amendment was adopted, the American Colonies had taken a very proactive stance regarding firearms. In many places, laws were enacted that required each family to arm themselves while attending church services.

There was a general feeling that a well-armed congregation would be better able to deal with any hostile force either at the Sunday worship service itself or traveling the actual route to and from Church.

In fact some churches used gunfire to summon nearby people to church. While it was more likely to hear a bell or some type of horn, there are accounts where the firing of a musket was the standard Sunday call to services.

Some of the guns-to-church laws merely alluded to a "serviceable gun, with sufficient power and shot." However other Colonial laws were a little more specific calling for a gun of militia use or "a pair of horse-pistols, in good order and fit for service."

Among the many guns-to-church laws of the American frontier in 1600s and 1700s, most made vague references of the need for "better security" in places of worship. Others made reference to hostiles or Indians. A 1743 law in South Carolina, however, made specific reference to possible insurrections "and other wicket attempts of Negroes and other slaves" as just cause for being fully armed in Church.

Despite the concerns and the peppering of such guns-to-church laws the punishment was usually just a simple fine payable to a church official. The fine was often divided between the church officer and the 'informer' who had reported the infraction.

Punishment however could be harsh if the blame of not bringing a weapon to church services could be laid upon a servant or slave. In such cases offender could be sentenced to as much as twenty lashes upon their bare shoulders.

Paxtang Church, Harrisburg, Pennsylvania.

Bruton Parish Church, Williamsburg, Virginia.

Virginia, 1643

One Fixed Gun

"It is enacted and confirmed, that masters of every family shall bring with them to church on Sundays one fixed and serviceable gun, with sufficient powder and shot, upon penalty of ten pounds of tobacco for every mast of a family so offending, to be disposed of by the church wardens, who shall levy it by distress.

"And servants being commanded and yet omitting, shall receive twenty lashes on his or their bare shoulders, by order from the county courts where he or they shall live."

South Carolina, 1743

Armed to Church

"Whereas, it is necessary to make some further provisions for securing the inhabitants of this province against insurrections and other wicked attempts of Negroes and other slaves within the same, we therefore humbly pray his most sacred majesty that it may be enacted, and be it enacted by Hon. William Bull, Esq., lieutenant-governor and commander-in-chief in and over his majesty's province of South Carolina, by and with the advice and consent of his majesty's honorable Council, and Commons House of Assembly of this province, and by the authority of the same.

"That within three months from the time of passing this act every white male inhabitant of this province (except travelers and such persons as shall be above sixty years of age) who, by the laws of this province, is or shall be liable to bear arms in the militia of this province, either in times of alarm or at common musters, who shall, on any Sunday or Christmas day in the year, go and resort to any church or any place of divine worship within this province, and shall not carry a gun or a pair of horse-pistols, in good order and fit for service, with at least six charges of gunpowder and ball, and shall not carry the same into the church or other place of divine worship as aforesaid, every such person shall forfeit and pay the sum of twenty shillings, current money, for every neglect of the same.

"The one-half thereof to the church-wardens of the respective parish in which the offense shall be committed, for the use of the poor of said parish, and the other half to him or them who will inform for the same, to be recovered on oath before any of his majesty's justices of the peace within this province in the same way and manner that debts under twenty pounds are directed to be recovered by the act for the trial of small and mean causes."

South Carolina, 1765

Carry Arms to Church

Presented by the grand jury, "as a grievance the want of a law to oblige the inhabitants of Charleston to carry arms to church on Sundays, or other places of worship."

Georgia, 1770

For Better Security

"An act for the better security of the inhabitants, by obliging the male white persons to carry fire-arms to all places of public worship."

Horse Stealing

orse stealing was a serious offense in early Colonial America, with a first offender just getting by with having an ear lopped off or a bare back whipping on the Public Square, but a second offender faced the death penalty.

There were literally hundreds of crimes punishable by the death penalty in Colonial America, but certain enacted laws at the time put stealing a cow, a chicken, or a horse right up there with armed robbery and murder.

Furthermore, horse stealing was also often punishable without the benefit of clergy.

That 'without benefit of clergy' did not mean, as some may interpret at first glance today, that the condemned would not have access of a spiritual leader. It was considerably more serious.

Under Old English law the term "benefit of clergy" originally provided that certain clergy, when charged with a crime, could seek to be tried by authorities within the church rather than the regular court system. Eventually it became a means in English courts where a first-time offender or an offender charged with a relatively minor crime might seek leniency by invoking the benefit of clergy.

In some cases it might merely mean paying a fine directly to the church rather than the court. Gradually it came to involve memorizing a passage of the Bible, usually a particular Psalm, and rendering it at sentencing. It was popular at a time when most people were illiterate, so it demonstrated a true effort at redemption.

By the late 1600s so-called lesser crimes in Colonial America were still generally allowed the lesser alternative of benefit of clergy, which meant basically a less severe punishment. Things took a harsher turn in the early 1700s, however, and even relatively minor crimes such as theft of a cow or stealing a horse, and other petty theft, became a felony in many of the providences — and some laws specifically spelled out that no benefit of clergy would be allowed.

The term itself remained a confusing one. It was entirely removed from the federal courts of the United States in 1790. However, it continued to be occasionally noted in state courts well into the middle of the nineteenth century.

Province of New Hampshire, 1679

Strangers or Inhabitants

"That if any strangers or inhabitants of this Province shall be legally convicted of stealing or purloining any horses, chattels, money, or other goods of any kind, he shall be punished by restoring three fold to the party wronged.

"And a fine or corporal punishment, as the court or three of the council shall determine. Provided that such sentence, where not given by the court, it shall be the liberty of the delinquent to appeal to the next court, putting in due caution there to appear and abide a trial."

Maryland, 1744

Horse Stealing

"All and every person and persons who shall hereafter feloniously take or steal any horse or horses, mare or mares, gelding or geldings, colt or colts, within this province, and all aiders, abettors and accessories, either before or after the fact, of any such takers or stealers, and all and every person who shall buy, take or receive any stolen horse, mare gelding, or colt, knowing the same to be feloniously taken or stolen;

"And shall be thereof convicted, by confession or verdict, or be outlawed, or will not upon arraignment, answer directly according to law, or shall willfully and of malice stand mute, or shall peremptorily challenge above twenty, shall for every such offense or offenses as aforesaid suffer death as a felon, without the benefit of clergy."

South Carolina, 1768

Loss of An Ear

"From and immediately after the passing of this act, all and every person and persons who shall be indicted and found guilty of stealing any horse, mare, gelding, colt or filly, shall, for the first offense, be punished with loss of an ear, and be publicly whipped, not exceeding thirty-nine lashes, on the bare back.

"And for the second offense shall be adjudged and deemed guilty of felony, and shall suffer death without the benefit of clergy."

18th century carriage, Williamsburg, Virginia

Idleness

Yes, as a matter of fact, it was a crime in Colonial America to be lazy.

It was not just a matter of social commentary about that 'worthless bum who has never done a day's worth of work.' It was a matter for community action.

Laws were very similar throughout the Colonies, often word for word. Many of the laws specifically instructed an authority figure in the community to seek out malingering persons whether local citizens or travelers. Usually such laws called for special attention to be paid to drifters, tobacco smokers, and those obviously not busy at work.

In some cases references were made in the laws to common coasters, unprofitable fowlers, and tobacco takers. Basically the coasters term in the 1600s made reference to young unemployed men who spent idle time along the shores of various towns fishing, chasing after birds, or just standing about and smoking. The coasting aspect of the term even then suggested moving about with no effort as in coasting down hill when sledding.

Smoking in public was considered distasteful during those times and generally decried by those of the ruling power. The act itself was considered a crime in some locations of the American Colonies.

Colonists tended to think that bad habits fell upon those who took up idleness.

As historian J. R. H. Moore observed of that era, "It was a most fortunate thing for the Colonies that so large a proportion of their settlers came from the middle and lower classes, from among men who thought it a disgrace and even sin not to work."

The rather overwhelming work ethic was ascribed in a large part to the teachings of sixteenth century reformer John Calvin, who considered a lack of productivity as bordering on evil.

"Idleness was Satan's opportunity; therefore it was only right that church members should reason with the weaker brethren who, by their idleness, gave Satan the chance to temp them," as Moore observed of that Calvinistic standard as it was held in the Colonies.

"Since crime and idleness went hand in hand," Moore added, "it was only proper that the community should have the right not only to punish crime, but to punish the very beginning of crime."

Pure and simple, under Colonial law, laziness was a crime.

Massachusetts, 1633

On Idleness

"It is ordered that no person, householder or other, shall spend time idly or unprofitably, under pain of such punishment as the county court shall think best to inflict.

"And the Constables of every town, are required to use special care and diligence to take knowledge of such offenders of this kind, especially of common coasters, unprofitable fowlers, and tobacco takers, and to present the same to the next magistrate, who is hereby empowered to her and determine the cause, or if the matter be of importance to transfer it to the Court."

Indians

olonial law dealt with the Native Americans on many levels and in many ways, from incredible cruelness to a condescending teaching of "civil and peaceable" behavior.

Colonials passed laws forbidding the selling of firearms or liquor to Indians, but prospered by providing both.

While the entire economy sometimes turned on the trade of blankets and trinkets for highly marketable furs and other animal skins, Colonial laws routinely forbade Indians from owning land or remotely having any equal status with white settlers.

The odd status of the Indian in the harsh and brutal climate of Colonial America is best illustrated in this quote from a Carolina law passed in 1719 before the region was divided into North and South Carolina. It read:

> "An Indian slave being reputed of much less value than a Negro, all persons possessed of Indian slaves shall pay for each Indian in proportion to half the value of what shall be rated and imposed for each Negro, and no more."

Some accounts suggest the Indians were ill adapted to the hard labors demanded by their Colonial taskmasters; other accounts indicate they were less healthy and more subject to illness or death. Others might argue that the Indians were naturally indigenous to the land and therefore more self-sufficient in adapting to their territory, and therefore less manageable as slave labor.

Historians Ernest Bogart and Donald Kemmerer simply conclude in their *Economic History of the American People*: "They (Indians) proved poor workers, however, and their place was soon taken by Negro slaves."

Be that as it may, the Indians were full partners in the fur trade, which would become a major Colonial industry. Generally white traders provided Indians with blankets, shirts, beads, ironware, trinkets, and various manufactured items in exchange for pelts or other animal skins.

"Due to the disparity place upon the value of the furs by the Indians and the white traders in terms of the commodities bartered by the latter," observe Bogart and Kemmer, "the trade was enormously profitable to the white man during the whole of the Colonial period."

In 1675, traders realized that relatively inexpensive beads at one dollar a pound and hatches at 75 cents each could be traded with the Indians for vast amounts of animal-bearing furs and skins. Those raw goods could then be shipped to England and other parts of the world to be sold at a significant profit. The delicate balance of such trading encouraged the establishment of more Colonial laws.

Two other elements woven into the vast landscape of trade with the Indians were liquor and firearms. One Colonial law after another forbade providing either of the two to the Indians and provided for severe penalties throughout the Colonies — and yet the practice prevailed.

Interestingly, it was, in part, the fur trade industry that prompted many Indian groups to move away from the more or less sedentary agricultural lifestyle of earlier days to more active hunting. That change in turn crafted further Indian interest in firearms and their potential.

Likewise, the fur trade industry exposed more and more Indians to the lure of liquor in general and rum in particular. The rivaling French could basically only offer brandy in trading with the Indians, imported from their native France, but many Indians considered brandy to be watery and inferior. The British, however, imported molasses from the West Indies to make plentiful supplies of rum throughout the Colonies, which led to rum becoming much more readily available for trading purposes. Rum was generally more favored by the unsuspecting Native Americans.

In July 1742, a Pennsylvania treaty between a Quaker group and the Indians included 60 kettles, 100 scissors, 1,000 tobacco pipes, 200 pounds of tobacco, and 25 gallons of rum. Historian J. R. Moore observed in the *Industrial History of People* that the large volume of rum was the last item on a long list of trade goods, "and they gave them the rum only after the bargain was concluded, not before."

Connecticut, 1650

Entering Homes

"It is ordered and decreed that where any company of Indians who sit down near any English Plantations, that they shall declare who is their Sachem or Chief, and that the said Chief or Sachem shall pay to the said English such trespasses as shall be committed by an Indian in the said plantation adjoining, either by spoiling or killing any Cattle or Swine, either with traps, dogs or arrows.

"And they were not to plead that it was done by strangers, unless they can produce the party and deliver him or his goods into custody of the English: And they shall pay double the damage if were done voluntarily.

"The like engagement this Court also makes to them in case of wrong or injury done to by the English, which shall be paid by the party by whom it was done, if thee can be made to appear, or otherwise by the Town in whose limits such acts are committed.

"For as much as our leniency and gentleness towards Indians has made them grow bold and insolent, to enter in Englishmen's houses, and unadvisedly handle swords and pieces and other instruments, many times to hazard the limbs or lives of English or Indians, and also to steal diverse goods out of such houses where they resort; for the presenting whereof, it is ordered that whatsoever Indian shall hereafter meddle with or handle any English man's weapons, of any sort, either in their houses or in the fields, they shall forfeit for every such default half a fathom of wampum; and if any hurt or injury shall thereupon follow to any persons life or limb, wound for wound, and shall pay for the healing of such wounds and other damages.

"And for anything they steal, they shall pay double, and suffer such further punishment as the Magistrates shall adjudge them. The Constable of any Town may attach and arrest any Indian that shall transgress in any such kind afore mentioned; and bring them before some Magistrate, who may execute the penalty of this order upon offenders; and may execute the penalty of this order upon offenders in an kind except life or limb, and any person that doth see such defaults may prosecute, and shall have half the forfeiture."

No Guns to Indians

"It is ordered by this Court and Authority thereof, that no man within this Jurisdiction shall, directly or indirectly, amend, repair, or cause to amended or repaired, any gun, small or great belonging to any Indian, nor shall endeavor the same; nor shall sell or give to any Indian, directly or indirectly, any such gun, nor gunpowder, or shot, or lead, or shot mould, or any military weapon or weapons, armor, or arrow heads; not sell nor barter nor give any dog or dogs, small or great.

"Upon pain of ten pounds fine for every offense, at least I any one of the aforementioned particulars; and the Court shall have power to increase the fine, or to impose corporal punishment where a fine cannot be had, at their discretion.

"And it is also ordered, that no person or persons shall trade with them at or about their wigwams, but in their vessels or places, or at their own houses, under penalty of twenty shillings for each default."

Living with Indians

"Whereas diverse persons depart from amongst us, and take up their abode with the Indians, in profane course of life; for the preventing where of.

"It is ordered that whatsoever person or persons that now inhabit, or shall in habit within this Jurisdiction, and shall depart from us and settle or join with the Indians, that they shall suffer three years imprisonment at least, in the House of Correction, and undergo such further censure, by fine or corporal punishment, the particular Court shall judge to inflict in such cases."

Massachusetts, 1700

Preventing Abuse of Indians

"Whereas, some of the principal and best disposed Indians within this province have represented and complained of the exactions and oppression, which some of the English exercise towards the Indians, by drawing them to consent to covenant or bind themselves or children apprentices or servants, for an unreasonable term, on pretense of or to make satisfaction for some small debt contracted or damages done by them.

"For redress whereof, be it enacted and declared by his Excellency the governor and the council and representatives in general court assembled, and by the authority of the same, that from now and after the publication of this act no Indian shall contract or put or bind him or herself, or child, apprentice or servant to any of his majesty's subjects, for any time or term of years, but by and with the allowance and approbation of two or more of his majesty's justices of the peace, who are required to take special care that the contract or covenant so be made, and the condition or terms thereof, be equal and reasonable both with respect to the time of service and otherwise.

"And be it further enacted, by the authority aforesaid, that the justices of the general sessions of the peace within the respective counties be and are hereby empowered, upon complaint made by any Indian native of this country, that is or shall be aggrieved by an indenture, covenant or agreement heretofore made by any time or term of service not yet expired, to hear and relieve such Indian according to justice and equity, and to regulate and order the time for such service as they shall judge reasonable."

Pennsylvania, 1701

Selling Liquor to Indians

"And forasmuch as several Sachems or Sachamacks, kings of the Indian nations, have, in their treaties with the proprietary and governor, earnestly desired that no Europeans should be permitted to carry rum to their towns because of the mischief before expressed, and since these evil practices plainly tend to the great dishonor of God, scandal of the Christian religion, and hindrance to the embracing thereof, as well as drawing the judgments of God upon the country if not timely prevented.

"For the prevention whereof for the future, be it further enacted, that if any person inhabiting in this province, or others, shall after the publication hereof, directly or indirectly sell, barter, give or exchange, by themselves or others, any rum, brandy or other spirits, mixed or unmixed, to or with any Indian within this province, and be legally convicted thereof, shall, for every such offense, forfeit ten pounds, one half to the use of the county wherein he is convicted and the other half to the discoverer and prosecutor, to be recovered in any court of record within this government."

Carolina, 1708

Indian Slaves

"Be it enacted by the authority aforesaid, that the captain or other person commanding-in-chief, commissioned for such an expedition, as aforesaid, is herby nominated and appointed commissioner to buy all prisoners of the said Indian enemies, above the age of twelve years, that shall be taken captive, either by white man or Indian, in the said expedition, as heretofore; and the salves so bought shall be taken care of and delivered by the said captain or other person commanding-in-chief, to the public receiver, who is hereby required and commanded to pay all such sum or sums of money that shall be drawn upon him by the commissioner aforesaid, for all such slave or slaves as he, the said commissioner, shall purchase, not exceeding the sum of seven pounds for every Indian slave.

"And the public receiver is hereby empowered to ship off to some islands of the West Indies the slaves so bought and delivered to him by the commissioner aforesaid, to be there sold, or disposed of them here, for the use of the public, to any person or persons who shall enter into the bonds, with the penalty of two hundred pounds, not to send or carry any slave or slaves so bought by him of them to any part or place within this province or to the northward thereof."

Massachusetts, 1712

Indians Prohibited

"An act prohibiting the importation or bring into this province any Indian servants or slaves.

"Whereas diverse conspiracies, barbarities, murders, thefts, and other notorious crimes and enormities, at sundry times and especially of late, have been perpetrated and committed by Indians and other slaves, within several of her majesty's plantations in America, being of a malicious, surly and revengeful spirit, rude and insolent in their behavior and very ungovernable; the over-great number and increase whereof within this province is likely to prove of pernicious and fatal consequence to her majesty's subjects and interests here, unless speedily remedied, and is a discouragement to the importation of white Christian servants, this province being differently circumstanced form the plantations in the islands, and having great numbers of the Indian natives of the country within and about them, and at this time under the sorrowful effects of their rebellion and hostilities.

"Be it therefore enacted by his Excellency, the governor, council and representatives, in general court assembled, and by the authority of the same, that, from and after the publication of this act, all Indians, male or female, of what age so ever, imported or brought into this province, shall be forfeited to his majesty for and towards the support of the government, unless the person or persons importing or bringing in such Indian or Indians shall give security at the secretary's office, of fifty pounds per head, to transport and carry out the same again within the space of one month next after their coming in, not to be returned to this province.

"And every master or other vessel, merchant or person whatsoever, importing or bringing into this province, by sea or land, any Indian or Indians, male or female, within the space of twenty-four hours next after their arrival or coming in, shall report and enter their names, number and sex, and give security in the secretary's office, as aforesaid, on pain of forfeiting to her majesty, for the support of the government, the sum of fifty pounds per head, to be used for and recovered in any of her majesty's courts of record by action, bill, complaint or information.

"And the fee to be paid for such entry and bond, as aforesaid, shall be two shillings and six pence, and no more."

Carolina, 1716

Captured Indian

"An Tuscarora Indian who shall, after ratification of this act, take captive any of our Indian enemies, shall have given up to him, in the room thereof, one Tuscarora Indian slaves."

Maryland, 1717

Indians Not Admitted

"Whereas, it may be of dangerous consequence to admit and allow as evidence in law in any of the courts of record, or before any magistrate within this province, any Negro or mulatto slave or free Negro, or mulatto born of a white woman, during their servitude appointed by law, or any Indian slave, or free Indian natives of this or the neighboring provinces.

"Be it therefore enacted by the right honorable the lord proprietary, by and with the advice and consent of his lordship's governor, and the upper and lower houses of Assembly, and by the authority of the same, that from and after the end of the present session of Assembly, no Negro or mulatto slave, free Negro, or mulatto born of a white woman, during his time of servitude by law, or any Indian salve, or free Indian natives of this or the neighboring provinces, be admitted and received as good and valid evidence in law in any matter or thing whatsoever pending before any court of record or before any magistrate within this province wherein any Christian white person is concerned."

Carolina, 1718

Assisting Cherokees

"An act to empower the honorable governor, to raise forces to be sent to the assistance of the Cherokees against their enemies.

"Further the safety of the province does, under God, depend on the friendship of the Cherokees to this government, which is in daily danger of being lost to us by the war now carried on against them by diverse nations of Indians, supported by the French, with a design to reduce them to obedience and dependence of that enterprising nation."

Carolina, 1719

Half the Value

"An Indian slave being reputed of much less value than a Negro, all persons possessed of Indian slaves shall pay for each Indian in proportion to half the value of what shall be rated and imposed for each Negro, and no more."

South Carolina, 1721

Indian Punishment

"All and every justice of the peace in this province, upon due complaint made to them by any of the inhabitants of the same, shall have power, and they are hereby empowered, to order corporal punishment to be inflicted by a constable upon any Indian or Indians that shall be proved to have done manifest injury to such inhabitants, in case the said Indian shall refuse or neglect to make such satisfaction to the inhabitant or inhabitants as the said justice or justices shall award or direct."

New Hampshire, 1721

Prohibiting Trade with Indians

"Whereas, the eastern Indians have broke and violated all treaties of peace and friendship made with them, and insulted the eastern settlements, be it therefore enacted that whoever shall (after) the twentieth day of this instant, October, directly or indirectly have any trade or commerce by way of gift, barter, or exchange, or any other way whatsoever, with any of aforesaid eastern Indians, or shall supply them with any provision, clothing, guns, powder, shot, bullets, or any other goods, wares, or merchandise whatsoever, shall forfeit and pay the sum of five hundred pounds, and suffer twelve months imprisonment without bail or mainprise upon the first conviction.

"If any person convicted of trading with any of the aforesaid Indians shall be so hardy as to carry on a trade or commerce with these Indians, in a manner as aforesaid, he shall, upon a second conviction, be deemed a felon, and suffer the pains of death."

Provincial Council of Pennsylvania, 1731

Indians and Rum

"Concerning rum and the carry (of) it into the woods. The governor knows there are ill people amongst the Christians as well as amongst them (Indians) and what mischief is done he believes is mostly own to rum, and it should be prevented.

"He desired that no Christian should carry any rum to Shamokin, where he lives, to sell. When they want it they will send for it themselves; they would not be wholly deprived of it, but they would not have it brought by the Christians.

"He desires four men may allowed to carry some rum to Allegheny, to refresh the Indians when they return from hunting, and that none else be admitted to carry any. They also desire that some rum be lodged at Tulphhockin and Pextan, to be sold to them, that their women may not have too long a way to fetch it."

South Carolina, 1731

Powder and Bullets

"No Indian to be trusted by Indian traders for more that one pound of powder and four pounds of bullets."

Georgia, 1744

Murder of Indians

"Whereas, it has been represented that some Indians, in amity with this province, have been barbarously murdered, to the great scandal of society and the danger of involving this province in a bloody and expensive war, and there is reason to believe that several ill-disposed persons have not considered such inhuman actions in a proper light, but being influenced by the ill-grounded prejudices which ignorant minds are apt to conceive against persons different in color form themselves, and unaware of the consequences, have rather looked on those murders as meritorious.

"To discourage, therefore, as much as may be, such unchristian like and cruel practices, and to explain and set forth the greatest danger thereof, it is declared, that to murder any free Indian, in amity with this province, is, by law of the land, as penal, to all intents and purposes whatsoever, as to murder any white person."

Connecticut, 1750

Teaching Indians

"Whereas, the bringing of the Indians in this land to knowledge and obedience of the only true God and Savior of mankind, and the Christian faith, as well as to a civil and peaceable behavior, was one great end professed by the first settlers of this colony in obtaining the royal charter, which profession this court being always desirous in the manner to pursue.

"Therefore, be it enacted that the authority and selectmen of each town within there are any Indians living or residing, shall take care, and they are hereby directed to endeavor to assemble and convene such Indians annually, and acquaint them with the laws of government made for punishing such immoralities as they may be guilty of, and make them sensible that they are not exempted from the penalties of such laws any more than his majesty's other subjects in the colony are.

"Every Indian convicted of drunkenness in this colony shall forfeit and pay the sum of five shillings, or else be openly whipped on the naked body, not exceeding ten stripes for one offense, as the assistant or justice before whom such conviction is in shall in his discretion determine; and if an Indian of Indians shall labor or play on the Sabbath or Lord's Day, within the limits of any town in this colony, and be thereof duly convicted, every such Indian shall forfeit the sum of three shillings, or else sit in the stocks one hour, at the discretion of the authority before whom the conviction is made."

Imported Indians

"Be it further enacted by authority aforesaid, that all Indians, male or female, of what age so ever, imported or brought into this colony by sea or land, from any place whatever, to be disposed of, left, or sold, within this colony, shall be forfeited to the treasury of this colony, and may be seized and taken accordingly; unless the person or persons importing or bringing in such Indian or Indians shall give security to some naval officer in this colony of fifty pounds per head, to transport or carry out the same again, within the space of one month next after their coming, not to be returned back to this colony."

Virginia, 1755

Hostile Indians

"Whereas, diverse cruel and barbarous murders have been lately committed in the upper parts of this (Virginia) colony, by Indians supposed to be in the common interest of the French, without any provocation from us, and contrary to the laws of nature and nations, and they still continue in skulking parties to perpetrate their barbarous and savage cruelties, in the most base and treacherous manner, surprising, torturing, killing and scalping, not only our men, who live dispersedly in the frontiers, but also their helpless wives and children, sparing neither age nor sex.

"For prevention of which shocking inhumanities, and for repelling such malicious and detestable enemies, be it enacted by the lieutenant-governor, council and burgesses of this present General Assembly, and it is hereby enacted by the authority of the same, that the sum of ten pounds shall be paid by the treasurer of this colony, out of the public money in his hands, to any person or persons, party or parties, either in the pay of this colony, or other inhabitants thereof, for every male Indian enemy, above the age of twelve years, by him or taken prisoner, killed or destroyed, within the limits of this colony, at any time within the space of two years after the end of this session of the Assembly.

"This act further provides that the scalp of every Indian, so to be killed or destroyed, as aforesaid, shall be produced to the governor or commander-in-chief."

Massachusetts, 1758

Regulating Indians

"Be it enacted by the governor, council and house of representatives, that there be three proper persons appointed for the future by the court, near to every Indian plantation in this province, guardians to the said Indians in their respective plantations, who are hereby empowered from this day, to take into their hands the said Indian lands, and allot to the several Indians of the several plantations such parts of the said lands and meadows as shall be sufficient for their particular improvement from time to time during the continuance of this act.

"And the remainder, if any there be, shall be let out by the guardians of the said respective plantations for suitable persons, for a term not exceeding the continuance of this act; and such part of the income thereof as necessary shall be applied for the support of such proprietors, in their respective plantations, as may be sick or unable to support themselves; and the surplus thereof, if any there be, shall be distributed amongst them or their said guardians, and that the respective guardians aforesaid be hereby empowered and enabled, in their own names and in their capacities as guardians, to being forward and maintain any action or actions for any trespass or trespasses that may be committed on the said Indian land, and that any liberty obtained from any Indian or Indians for cutting off any timber, wood, or hay, milking pine trees, carrying off any ore or grain, or planting or improving said lands, shall not be any bar to said guardians in their said action or actions.

"Provided, that nothing in this act shall be understood to bar any person or persons from letting creatures run upon the said Indians unimproved land that lie common and contiguous to other towns and proprietors."

New Jersey, 1758

Dogs For Hunting Indians

"Whereas, the Indian enemy are a very private and secret enemy, and it has been thought dogs would be a great service, not only in discovering them in their secret retreats among the swamps, rocks and mountains, frequent in those parts, but also in assisting the troops in pursuing and attacking them.

"Therefore, be it enacted by the authority aforesaid, that it shall and may be lawful for the paymaster aforesaid to procure, upon the best terms he can, fifty good, large, strong and fierce dogs, and the same, so procured, to supply with food necessary for their subsistence, equal to ten men's allowance in quantity; which said dogs will be disciplined for and employed in the service in such manner as the said major, in conjunction with the commission officers, or the major part of them, shall think proper."

North Carolina, 1760

Indians As Slaves, Scalps

"For the greater encouragement of persons as shall enlist voluntarily to serve in the said companies, and other inhabitants of this province who shall undertake any expedition against the Cherokees and other Indians in alliance with the French, be it further enacted by the authority aforesaid, that each of the said Indians who shall be taken as a captive, during the present war, by an person aforesaid, shall and his hereby declared to be a slave, and the absolute right and property of who shall be the captor of such Indian, and shall and may be possessed, pass, and remain to such captor, his executors, administrators and assigns, as a chattel personal.

"And if any person or persons, inhabitant or inhabitants of this province, not in actual pay, shall kill an enemy Indian or Indians, he or they shall have and receive ten pounds for each and every Indian he or they shall so kill; and any person or persons who shall be in the actual pay of this province shall have and receive five pounds for every enemy Indian or Indians he or they shall so kill, to be paid out of the treasury, any law, usage or custom to the contrary notwithstanding.

"Provided, always, that any person claiming the said reward, before he be allowed or paid the same, shall produce to the Assembly the scalp of every Indian so killed, and make oath or otherwise prove he was the person who killed, or was present at the killing of the Indian whose scalp shall be so produced, and that he hath not before had or received any allowance form the public for the same; and as a further encouragement, shall also have and kept to his or their own use or uses all plunder taken out of the possession of any enemy Indian or Indians, or within twenty miles of any of the Cherokee towns, or any Indian town at war with any of his majesty's subjects."

Liars

In Colonial America laws, liars did not necessarily mean the gossiping or bragging loudmouth of the village. It could be the more serious offender whose 'untruths' threatened to hamper the royal order of things.

One Colonial law dealing with divulgers of false news warned that some lies could be "pernicious" or highly injurious or destructive to the commonwealth. Still another Colony enacted a law about liars that made reference to the "liege," drawing distantly on a feudal allegiance between the peasants and lord of the realm.

Certainly such laws threatening to punish "any lie" could be interpreted as a significant roadblock to free speech. In fact free speech, as it is practiced in this era of America's existence, was not present in the pre-Revolutionary days of the Colonies.

Under stern British rule most Colonists were under ominous restrictions of the seditious libel laws that were enacted by English Parliament as far back as 1275. Basically those acts outlawed the telling or publishing of any so-called "false news or tales" that would create discord between the King and the people of the kingdom.

At the same time some experts today have argued that early American Colonists enjoyed limited freedom of comment and criticism that was clearly not available back in England. Others would point to the trial of John Peter Zenger for seditious libel much later in 1735 as a benchmark for a shadowy and mild freedom of speech. Zenger was not convicted of the crime, but then again it was not a matter of lying or false news reports.

A further complication was that different Colonies appeared to deal with "false news" at different levels.

During the latter 1600s the Virginia Colony noted "many idle and busy-headed people" were going about disturbing the peace with falsehoods, which were troubling to the country. However a law in New Hampshire instead dealt with "damage or hurt of any particular person" resulting a liar's deception.

In most cases the punishment, at least initially, in the Colonies was a fine or merely a spell at sitting in the public stocks. However it could sometimes escalate depending on the seriousness of the falsehood.

In one 1654 case, the Assembly of Virginia sought a somewhat different remedy. It seems that one William Hatcher had "maliciously reported" speaker of the house Col. Edward Hill to be "an atheist and blasphemer, and the mouth of his house was a devil," according to information exhibited against him the last quarter court, from which the honorable governor and council then cleared the said Col. Edward Hill.

Accordingly the offending Hatcher was ordered "upon his knees, to make a humble acknowledgement of his offense unto Col. Hill and the burgesses of this Assembly." That done Hatcher was dismissed, "after paying fees."

Virginia, 1662

Divulgers of False News

"Whereas, many idle and busy-headed people do forge and divulge false rumors and reports, to the great disturbance of the peace and quite of his Majesty's liege persons in this Colony.

"Be it enacted, that what person or persons so ever shall forge and divulge any such false reports tending to the trouble of the country, shall be by the next justice of the peace set for and bound over the next county court, where, if he produce not his author, he shall be fined two thousand pounds of tobacco (or less, if the court thinks fit to lessen it), and besides give bond for his behavior if it appears to the court that he did maliciously publish or invent it."

New Hampshire, 1679

Age 16 or Older

"It is enacted by this Assembly that what person so ever, being 16 years of age, or upward, shall wittingly or willingly make or publish any lie which may be tending to the damage or hurt of any particular person, or with intent to deceive and abuse the people with false news or reports.

"Shall be fined for every such default 10 shillings, and if the party cannot or will not pay the fine, then he shall sit in the stocks as long as the court shall think necessary; and if the offenders shall come to any one of council aforesaid to execute the law where he liveth, and spare his appearance in the Court, but in case when the lie is greatly pernicious to the commonwealth, it shall be more severely punished according to the nature of it."

Punishment

I n a very dark sense, early Colonists were most generous with punishment.

They seemed eager and enthusiastic to turn to branding, the ducking stool, the pillory, cutting off ears, whipping, hanging, or otherwise punish those deemed deserving of such treatment.

For the most part, such punishment was based on criminal codes enacted to strictly control citizen behavior, but they could be harsh. As one observer wrote in a 1624 letter, "some were laws written in blood."

Author and historian John Dillon was one of the first to fully comment on the situation in *Oddities of Colonial Legislation* written in 1879.

"Among the ways of inflicting punishment on the violators of early Colonial laws in America, were fines, imprisonment, banishment, standing in the pillory, whipping on the bare back, standing under the gallows with a rope around the neck, sitting in a cage, dunking, cutting off one ear, or both ears, branding on the forehead, boring the tongue with an hot iron, hanging, and dismemberment."

Dillon added:

"Even in the Province of Pennsylvania there were penal laws which provided for punishing criminals by burning in the hand, cutting off the ears, nailing an ear to the pillory, whipping, or imprisonment for life."

To understand the level of zeal and intensity felt by those in control of law and order in the Colonies, it is important to consider the heavy influence of the Old Country.

As the American Colonies were being formed and regulated, Europe was maintaining relatively severe standards for dealing with criminals. In England and other countries, people were routinely imprisoned for refusing to accept certain religious doctrines. Still others were imprisoned for debt and many relatively minor crimes, including repeated petty theft, were punishable by death.

Pilgrim stockade, Plymouth, Massachusetts.

The Public Gaol   *Williamsburg, V*

Early eighteenth century prison, Williamsburg, Virginia.

Generally the criminal codes 'imported' to the Colonies were slightly less extreme perhaps, but still shocking by modern terms.

Historian Fremont Wirth observed that even what Colonists considered less formal and less breath-taking punishments were "no less effective."

Among them were "those which required the offender to appear on the Sabbath day to confess his guilt before congregation, or which required that the effigy of the offender, tarred and feathered, be drawn through the streets. For those guilty of more serious crimes, cruel punishments were devised; counterfeiters and runaway servants might be branded or have their ears cut off; and the gallows, standing in public place, served as a constant warning to murders and pirates."

Branding, as we have seen, was a Colonial standard. In some Colonial locations it could be administered for everything from adultery to witchcraft. However, usage, and even purpose of the individual letter, varied somewhat by region.

Typically the letter "A" was branded upon a person said to have committed adultery, "B" was for burglar, "F" for forgery, "H" for hog or horse stealing, "M" for manslaughter, "R" for rogue, "SL" for seditious libel, "T" for thief, and so forth.

The specific area on the body where the brand was placed also varied. It could be one or both hands. It could also be one or both cheeks of the face, or simply on the forehead.

Such resulting disfigurement might be shocking to people today, but Dr. Lawrence M. Friedman has pointed out in *History of American Law* that it was hardly cause for alarm in Colonial times.

"The sight of a man lopped of his ears, or slit of his nostrils, or with a seared brand or great gash in his forehead or cheek could not affect the stout stomachs that cheerfully and eagerly gathered around the bloody whipping post and gallows," Friedman wrote.

These whipping posts, gallows, and pillories were always fairly near for the crowd's gatherings. In many of the Colonies, nearly every community had stocks, whipping posts, a pillory, and accompanying brand irons. Such facilities, like the public parks of today, were well maintained and frequently in use.

Ironically, as it may seem in the Colonial land of no nonsense in dealing with crime, it is interesting to note that some so-called criminals were actually imported from England.

As previously indicated, people in England during that same period were being imprisoned for their debts, and could be put to death for stealing property of relatively little value. Gradually the English courts developed an option for their growing number of criminals — send them to the American Colonies.

"The people of the Colonies were greatly in need of help to develop their natural resources, while so many people of England were in great distress from lack of work," according to the writings of historian J. R. H. Moore, who also noted:

"The rich dreaded the great expense of enforcing their poor laws, and the poor found little but hardship in (English) life.

"So in order to show mercy to a man arrested for stealing, the prisoner was charged with having stolen property to the value of five shillings and eleven pence — rather than the death punishable amount of six shillings; the judge could then sentence him to transportation (to the Colonies), and a strong man, who probably was not a criminal by instinct, was saved to perform for the country valuable service in the Colonies."

Then too there was the benefit of clergy clause.

Back in twelfth century England the term benefit of clergy actually provided that members of the clergy were exempt from criminal prosecution for felonies in English courts. Instead they were to be prosecuted and if need be punished under jurisdiction of the Church.

Over time other accused criminals sometimes posed as members of the clergy to obviously save themselves from the more serious punishment of acting English courts, which could include the gallows. Often times that impersonation involved the reading of a passage from the Christian Bible if a suspect was literate enough to read it. Eventually word filtered down even into the Colonies that even non-readers could memorize a Bible passage and gain a moderation in punishment.

Early in the 1700s the reading or memorizing part of the law was abolished, and usually criminals were simply allowed to claim benefit of clergy upon the first conviction of a felony. Colonial laws, however, specifically stated in certain crimes that the so-called benefit of clergy was not permitted.

In 1718, British law assured that those who pleaded benefit of clergy could be sentenced if necessary to seven years banishment to the Colonies. Thus they joined the other 'imported' criminals going to the New World.

Later in 1790 an Act of Congress removed the benefit of clergy clause entirely from the Federal courts of America. It remained still in use, however, in some state courts.

Aside from a few modifications on both sides of the ocean, punishment under Colonial law was chilling.

Legendary preacher Cotton Mather once witnessed the hanging of a convicted rapist and the burning of two black servants who had earlier burned houses and their occupants. Mediating on the gruesome penalties Mather condemned then-seventeenth century Massachusetts's governor William Bradford for it. He reminded Bradford that the governor's heart contained inclinations, which would make him too "as vile as the vilest, if sovereign grace did not prevent it."

Centuries later historian Friedman more or less confirmed it, saying, "The earliest criminal codes mirrored the nasty, precarious life of pioneer settlements."

Massachusetts, 1646

Interrupting Preaching

"Forasmuch as the open contempt of God's Word, and messengers thereof, is the desolating sin of civil states and churches; it is ordered, that if any Christian within this jurisdiction shall contemptuously behave himself toward the word preached, or the messengers thereof called to dispense the same in any congregation, when he doth faithfully execute his service and office therein according to the will and word of God, either by interrupting him in his preaching, or by charging him falsely with any error which he hath not taught in the open face of the church.

"Or, like a son of Korah, cast upon his true doctrine, or himself, any reproach to the dishonor of the Lord Jesus, who hath sent him, and to the disparagement of his holy ordinance, making God's ways contemptible and ridiculous; that every such person or persons shall, for the first scandal, be convened and reproved openly by the magistrate at some lecture, and bound to their good behavior.

"And if a second time they break forth into the like contemptuous carriages they shall either pay five pounds to the treasury, or stand two hours openly on a block or stool four foot high, on a lecture day, with a paper fixed on his breast, written in capital letters, 'An Open and Obstinate Contemner of God's Holy Ordinances,' that others may hear and be ashamed of breaking out into like wickedness."

Virginia, 1662

Putting on the Pillory

"Whereas, many offenses are publishable by the laws of England and of this country with corporal punishments, for executing whereof no such provision hath been made as the aid laws do require.

"Be it therefore enacted, that in every county the court cause to be set up a pillory, a pair of stocks and a whipping-post, near the court house, and a ducking-stool in such a place as they shall think convenient, that such offenders as by the laws are to suffer by any of them may be punished according to their demerits.

"And the courts not causing the said pillory and whipping-post, stocks and ducking-stool to be erected within six months after this date, shall be fined five thousand pounds of tobacco to the use of the public."

Massachusetts, 1672

No Torture, Or Some

"And no man shall be forced by torture to confess any crime against himself, or any other, unless he is first fully convicted by clear and sufficient evidence to be guilty, after which if the case be of that nature that it is very apparent there be other conspirators or confederates with him, then he may be tortured.

"Yet not with such tortures as are barbarous and inhumane."

Virginia, 1723

Off With Their Ears

"And to the end such Negroes, mulattoes or Indians, not being Christians, as shall hereafter be produced as evidences, on the trail of any slave for capital crimes, may be under the greater obligation to declare the truth.

"Be it enacted, that where any such Negro, mulatto or Indian shall, upon due proof made, or pregnant circumstances appearing before any county court within this colony, be found to have given a false testimony, every such offender shall, without further trial, be ordered by the said court to have one ear nailed to the pillory, and there to stand for the space of one hour, and then the said ear to be cut off; and thereafter, the other ear nailed in like manner, and cut off at the expiration of one other hour.

"And moreover, to order every such offender thirty-nine lashes, well laid, on his or her bare back, at the common whipping-post.

"And be it further enacted, that at every such trial of slaves committing capital offenses, the person who shall be first named in the commission sitting on such trial, before the examination of every Negro, mulatto or Indian, not being a Christian, charge such evidence to declare the truth; which charge shall be in the words following:

"You are brought hither as a witness, and, by the direction of the law, I am to tell you, before you give your evidence, that you must tell the truth, the whole truth, and nothing but the truth; and that if it be found hereafter that you tell a lie and give false testimony in this matter, you must, for so doing, have both your ears nailed to the pillory, and cut off, and receive thirty-nine lashes on your base back, well laid on, at the common whipping-post."

Rogues

During the middle 1500s, the English began using the term "rogue" to describe shiftless people who wandered the countryside being a nuisance.

In the American Colonies, where laws were used to deal with just about every situation, there was an effort to outlaw rogues. Sometimes the Colonial laws were broadened in an attempt to include just about any unsavory person appearing on the horizon of the community.

For instance, some of the laws specifically made reference to vagabonds, idle persons (see "*Idleness*"), fortunetellers, jugglers, fiddlers, story-tellers, runaways, unruly children, beggars, those swearing in public, and otherwise anyone else who on the horizon of the community did not fit into its social standards.

Punishment, given the Colonial temperament and intolerance, was relatively mild. Usually it involved spending time in a house of correction; mainly it was to rid the community of what authorities determined to be an unwanted annoyance.

Connecticut, 1750

Begging Your Pardon

"An act for restraining, correcting, suppressing and punishing rogues, vagabonds, common beggars, and other lewd, idle, dissolute, profane and disorderly persons, and for setting them to work.

"And it shall and may be lawful for the respective county courts in this Colony, and for an assistant and justice of the peace, or two justices of the peace to apprehend, send and commit to such houses of correction, to be kept and governed there according to the rules and orders of such houses, respectively, all rogues, vagabonds, and idle persons going from place to place begging.

"Also all persons using, or pretending to use, any subtle craft, juggling, or unlawful games or plays, or feigning themselves to have knowledge of physiognomy, palmistry, or pretending they can tell destinies, fortunes, or discover where lost or stolen goods may be found.

"Also common pipers, fiddlers, runaways, stubborn servants or children, common drunkards, common night walkers, pilferers, wanton and lascivious persons, either in speech or behavior, common railers or brawlers.

"Also such as are guilty of reviling and profane speaking, or neglect their calling, misspend what they earn, and do not provide for themselves or the support of their families, upon due conviction of any of the offenses or disorders aforesaid."

At "Shirley" on the James River,

June 23/1909.   As Ever H.S.

Shirley Manor House, James River, Virginia.

Sabbath Breakers

I t would be difficult to overestimate the emphasis early Colonists put on not only attending Church services on Sunday, but also not engaging in any Sunday activity that would distract from the sanctity of the Lord's Day. Those who chose to do other things rather than observe the religious tradition were declared to be Sabbath Breakers.

There were accounts that in some Colonial locations authorities were known to have searched for would-be parishioners in their homes. Those that were found, unless they proved to be sick, were commanded to appear for church services. Historian Alice Morse Earl, writing in *Home Life in Colonial Days* suggests some early Colonial leaders even considered threat of the death penalty for certain Sabbath Breakers, "but this severity never was executed."

Generally the Colonial laws prohibited working and traveling during Sunday. Many also prohibited fishing, hunting, gaming, shooting, sports, playing, or most any other type of recreation throughout the Lord's Day.

Violators or Sabbath Breakers were usually subject to fines and periods in the stockades on the public square. However imprisonment and further punishment could sometimes be applied if the offenses seemed to be especially uncaring and reckless.

Virginia, 1629

Attend Church

"It is ordered that there be especial care taken by all commanders and others that the people do repair to their churches on the Sabbath day, and to see that the penalty of one pound of tobacco for every time of absence, and fifty pounds for every month's absence, set down in the act of the General Assembly, be levied and the delinquents to pay the same, as also to see that the Sabbath day be not ordinarily profaned by working in any employments or by journeying from place to place."

New Jersey, 1675

Unlawful Recreations

"It is enacted by this Assembly that whosoever shall profane the Lord's Day, otherwise called Sunday, by any kind of servile work, unlawful recreations or unnecessary travels on that day not falling within the compass of works or mercy or necessity, either willfully or through careless neglect, shall be punished by fine, imprisonment or corporally, according to the nature of the offense, at the judgment of the court, justice of justices where the offense is committed."

New Jersey, 1677

Sunday Peace

"All constables are hereby required, if upon their own knowledge they shall be privy to any such disorders on Sunday by sight or information thereof, to repair to the said place, and, finding any person or persons misbehaving themselves, namely, staggering, reeling, drinking, cursing, swearing, quarreling or singing any vain songs, or tunes of the same, shall cause the said person or persons to be set in the stocks for two whole hours without relief."

New Hampshire, 1680

High Handed Sin

"Upon information of sundry abuses and misdemeanors committed by diverse persons on the Lord's Day, it is therefore ordered and enacted by this General Assembly, that what person so ever within this Government shall profane the Lord's Day, by doing unnecessary work or travel, or by sports or recreations, or by being at ordinaries (taverns) in time of public worship, such person or persons shall forfeit 10 shillings, or be whipped for every such offense.

"And if it appears that the sin was proudly or presumptuously, and with a high hand, committed against the known command and authority of the Blessed God, such person therein despising and reproaching the Lord, shall be severely punished at the Judgment of the Court."

OLD ST. JOHN'S CHURCH (BROAD AND TWENTY-FIFTH STREETS), RICHMOND, VA.

St. John's Church, Richmond, Virginia.

St. Paul's Episcopal Church, Norfolk, Virginia.

Carolina, 1691

No Worldly Labor

"Forasmuch as there is nothing more acceptable to Almighty God than the true, sincere performance of and obedience to the most divine service and worship, which, although at all times, yet chiefly upon the Lord's Day, commonly called Sunday, ought so to be done.

"But instead thereof many idle, loose and disorderly people do willfully profane the same in tippling, shooting, gaming, and many other exercises, pastimes and meetings, whereby ignorance prevails and the just judgment of Almighty God may reasonably be expected to fall upon this land if the same by some good orders be not prevented.

"Be it enacted that no tradesman, artificer, workman, laborer, or any other person whatsoever, shall use or exercise any worldly labor, business or work of their ordinary calling on the Lord's Day or any part thereof, works of necessity or charity only excepted.

"And that every person being of sixteen years or upwards offending in the premises, shall, for every such offense, forfeit the sum of five shillings for each person every day.

"And that no person or persons whosoever shall publicly cry, cal forth or expose to sale or sell any wares, merchandise, fruits, herbs, goods or chattels whosoever, upon the Lord's Day or any part thereof, upon pain every person so offending shall forfeit the said goods so cried and show forth or exposed to sale or sold.

"In case of the default or inability of offending persons to pay such fines or forfeitures then the party offending do set publicly in the stocks for the space of two hours."

New Hampshire, 1700

No Work or Travel

"Be it enacted and ordained by the lieutenant governor, council, and representatives, convened in General Assembly, and it is enacted by the authority of the same, that all and every person and persons whatsoever, shall, on that day carefully apply themselves to duties of religion and piety, publicly and privately.

"And that no tradesman, artificer, or other person whatsoever, shall, upon the land or water, do or exercise any labor, business, or work of their ordinary calling, nor use any game, sport, play or recreation on the Lord's Day, or any part thereof, with works of necessity and mercy only excepted, upon pain that every person so offending shall forfeit five shillings.

"Further, it is ordered and declared, that no traveler, drover, horse-courser, waggoner, butcher, haggler, or any of their servants, shall travel on that day, or any part thereof, except by some adversity they were belated and forced to lodge in the woods, wilderness or highways the night before, and in such case to travel no further than the next inn or place of shelter on that day, upon penalty of twenty shillings."

Carolina, 1712

Travel Prohibited

"Be it enacted, by the authority aforesaid, that no drover, waggoner, butcher, haggler, they or any of their servants, or any other traveler or person whatsoever, shall travel on the Lord's Day by land, neither shall any person or persons whatsoever travel on the Lord's Day by water in any barge, lighter, boat, canoe, or periauger, excepting it be to go to the place of religious worship and return again, or to visit or relieve any sick person, or unless the person or persons were belated the night before, and then to travel no further than to some convenient inn or place of shelter for that day, or upon extraordinary occasion, for which he, she or they shall be allowed to travel under the hand of some justice of the peace of this province."

Maryland, 1723

Slaves Included

"Be it enacted, that no person whatsoever shall work or do any bodily labor on the Lord's Day, commonly called Sunday, and that no person, having children, servants, or slaves, shall wittingly or willingly suffer any of them to do any manner of work or labor on the Lord's Day, works of charity always excepted.

"Nor shall suffer or permit children, servants, or slaves, to profane the Lord's Day, by gaming, fishing, fowling, hunting, or unlawful pastimes or recreation, and that every person transgressing this act, and being thereof convicted, by the oath of one sufficient witness, or confession of the party before a single magistrate, shall forfeit two hundred pounds of tobacco, to be levied and applied as aforesaid."

Georgia, 1762

Football Playing

"Working, hunting, fishing, bull-baiting, bear-baiting, horse racing, football playing, or other games, exercises, sports or pastimes whatsoever are prohibited on the Lord's Day, five shillings penalty for every such offense."

Schooling

E ducating children in the early American Colonies came in many shades. Some locations delighted in it while other locations detested the mere thought of such an endeavor.

At one point during the seventeenth century the British commissioners made some inquiries as to how the various English Colonies were dealing the idea of schooling for at least some of their youngsters.

The governor of Connecticut, in his reply, offered, "One-fourth of the annual revenue of the Colony is laid out in maintaining free schools for the education of our children."

Meanwhile, the terse reply from the governor of Virginia to the British commissioners was in stark contrast, "I thank God that there are no free schools nor printing, and I hope we shall not have these (for a) hundred years; for learning has brought disobedience, and heresy, and sects in the world, and printing has divulged them, and libels against the best government. God keep us from both."

Obviously the early Colonies were not allied when it came to schooling. Their attitudes and consequently their laws sometimes reflected these viewpoints.

Generally the people of the New England Colonies were anxious for their children to learn the basics of reading and writing. In 1642, an act of the General Court pointed out there was a "great neglect in many parents and masters in training up their children in learning and labor... especially of the ability to read and understand the principles of religion and the capital laws of the country."

Prior to the establishment of public schools, small children were often sent to the homes of some of the local women where they were taught the alphabet and a few words. Some of these early arrangements were known as dame schools. Later more regular schools became known as public schools.

The early Colonial legislatures in many cases assumed large responsibility for the establishment and maintenance of public schools. The Massachusetts General Assembly took the lead in progressive education legislation, and the law passed in 1647 — sometimes known as the Old Deluder Satan Act — is still regarded by many historians and educators as the most important school law ever to be passed in American history.

Basically the Satan Act, figuring idle time worked in favor of Satan, required every township having fifty householders to provide a teacher and school building where children were to be taught to read and write. Other New England Colonies later duplicated it.

There were some problems however. For one thing, although the townships were subject to a fine for non-compliance, sometimes the law was ignored locally. Further, while these early Massachusetts schools were public in the sense they were open to all, they were free only to the children of very poor parents. Other parents or even the township had to bear certain costs.

Finally, not all the Colonies were as eager to provide schooling as Massachusetts.

"South of the Potomac, education lagged far behind the New England example," observe Richard Wade, Howard Wilder, and Louise Wade in the textbook, *A History of the United States*. "There was not strong religious motive to establish schools. Moreover, people were widely scattered on plantations and farms, thus making it difficult to bring teachers and students together."

They added:

> "Old field schools, on worn-out plantation lands, taught the basic elements of reading and writing to some white children, but most of the plantations hired private tutors. In the southern cities, the children were taught in academies and dame schools held in private homes. Children of poorer parents attended charity schools or went without an education."

In contrast to Massachusetts in particular and New England, a group of generally middle Colonies such as New York, Pennsylvania, New Jersey, Delaware, and Maryland tended toward a more church-related type of schooling. Often various dominations operated their schools in connection with their church. More church ritual was incorporated along with the basic reading and writing.

A third alternative was generally represented in the southern Colonies; they tended to follow the New England system of education in some ways. However they did not encourage such a wide plan of free elementary schooling for all children. Instead they favored private secondary schools and colleges under public patronage.

Historians have made note of a few scattered attempts among the southern Colonies to compel education attendance, and to provide a tax-supported county system of school. In some cases so-called pauper schools were provided for poor children in larger centers. Often such schooling was lead by indentured white servants who lacked training as a teacher.

Sometimes the indentured servants literally fled the responsibility of children and schooling. *The Maryland Gazette* of February 28, 1771 contained an advertisement that read in part: "Ran away, a servant man, from Dorchester County, who had followed the occupation of a schoolmaster; much given to drink and gambling."

In the same newspaper, this one dated 1774, a related advertisement appears:

"To be sold, a schoolmaster and indented servant, who has got two years to serve. He is sold for not fault, not more than we are done with him. He can learn bookkeeping, and is an excellent good scholar."

Of course in other places schoolmasters were hired for the specific task of teaching. In some cases they were paid by the parents or by the masters of such children, or even by the general population of a village or plantation.

Massachusetts, 1642

Education of Children

"Forasmuch as the good education of children is of singular behoove and benefit to any commonwealth; and whereas many parents and masters are too indulgent and negligent of their duty in this kind.

"It is therefore ordered by this court and the authority thereof, that he selectmen of every town, in the several precincts and quarters where they dwell, shall have a vigilant eye over their brethren and neighbors to see, first, that none of them shall suffer so much barbarism in any of their families as not to endeavor to teach, by themselves or others, their children and apprentices so much learning as may enable them perfectly to read the English tongue and knowledge of the capital laws, upon penalty of twenty shillings for each neglect therein.

"And further, that all parents and masters do breed and bring up their children and apprentices in some honest, lawful calling, labor or employment, either in husbandry or some other trade, profitable to themselves and the commonwealth. If they will not nor cannot train them to fit them for higher employments, and if any of the selectmen, after admonition by them given to such masters of families, shall find them negligent of their duty in the particulars aforementioned, whereby children and servants become rude, stubborn and unruly, the said selectmen, with the help of two magistrates, shall taken such children or apprentices form them and place them with some masters for years — boys till they come to twenty-one and girls eighteen years of age, complete, which will more strictly look unto and force them to submit unto governments, according to the rules of the order, if by fair means and former instructions they will not be drawn into it."

Connecticut, 1650

Satan Waiting

"It being of chief project of that Old Deluder, Satan, to keep men from the knowledge of the Scriptures, as in former times keeping them in an unknown tongue, so in these latter times by persuading them from the use of Tongues, so that at least the true sense and meaning of the original might be clouded with false glosses of saint seeming deceivers; and that Learning may not be buried in the Grave of our Forefathers, in Church and Common wealth, the Lord assisting our endeavors.

"It is therefore ordered by this Court and Authority there of, that every Township within this Jurisdiction, after the Lord hath increased them to the number of fifty householders, shall then forthwith appoint one within their Towne to teach all such children as shall report to him, to write and read, whose wages shall be paid either by the parents or masters of such children, or by the inhabitants in general by way of supply, as the major part of those who order the prudential of the Towne shall appoint.

"Provided that those who send their children be not oppressed by more than they can have them taught in other Towns.

"And it is further ordered, that where any Town shall increase to the number of one hundred families or householders, they shall set up a Grammar School, the masters thereof being able to instruct youths so far as they may be fitted for the University.

"And if any Town neglect the Performance hereof above one year, then every such Towne shall pay five pounds per annum, to the next such School, till they shall perform this order."

Provincial Council of Pennsylvania, 1683

Philadelphia Schoolmaster

"The governor and council, having taken into their serious consideration the great necessity there is for a schoolmaster, for the instruction and education and sober education of youth in the town of Philadelphia, sent for Enoch Flower, an inhabitant of the said town, who for twenty years past hath been exercised in that care and employment in England, to whom having communicated their minds, he embraced it upon the following terms:

"To learn to read English, four shillings by the quarter; for boarding a scholar, that is to say, diet, washing, lodging and schooling, ten pounds for one whole year."

New Jersey, 1693

New Jersey Schoolmasters

"Whereas, the cultivating of learning and good manners tends greatly to good and benefit of mankind, which has hitherto been much neglected in this province.

"Be it therefore enacted by the by the governor, council and deputies, in General Assembly now met and assembled, and by the authority of the same, that the inhabitants of any town within this province shall and may by warrant from a justice of the peace of that county, when they think fit and convenient, meet together and make choice of three more men of the said town, to make a rate for the salary and maintaining of a schoolmaster within the said town, for so long a time as they think fit.

"And the consent and agreement of the major part of the inhabitants of said town shall bind and oblige the remaining part of the inhabitants of the said town to satisfy and pay their shares and proportion of the said rate; and in case of refusal or non-payment, distress to be made upon the goods and chattels of such person or persons so refusing or not paying, by the constable of the said town, by virtue of a warrant from a justice of the peace of that county, and the distress so taken to be sold at a public venue, and the surplus, if any be after payment of the said rate and charges, to be returned to the owner."

Carolina, 1710

Free School

"Whereas, it is necessary that a free school be erected for the instruction of youth of this province in grammar and other arts and religion; and whereas, several charitable and well disposed Christians, by their last wills and testaments, have given several sums of money for the founding of a free school, but no person has yet is authorized to take charge and care of erecting a free school, according to the intent of the of the donors, and to receive said legacies, if tendered, nor to demand the same, incase of refusal to pay the same.

"So that, for want of some person or persons or body politic and corporate, proper for the lodging the said legacies, therein, the same are not applied according to the pious and charitable intention of the testators or donors."

*The act further appointed commissioners to govern such funding.

New Hampshire, 1714

Every Town

"It is enacted and ordered, that for building and repairing of meeting houses, ministers' houses and school houses, and allowing a salary to a schoolmaster of each town within this province, the selectmen, in their respective towns, shall raise money by an equal rate and assessment upon the inhabitants, in the same manner as in this present act directed for the maintenance of the minister.

"And every town within this province, shall, form and after the publication hereof; provide a schoolmaster for the supply of the town."

New Hampshire, 1719

Master Procured

"Be it enacted that every town with in this province, having the number of fifty householders or upward, shall be constantly provided of a schoolmaster to teach children and youth to read and write.

"And where any town or towns have the number of one hundred families, or householders, there shall also be a grammar school set up and kept in every such town, and some discreet person, of good conversation, well instructed in the tongues, shall be procured as master thereof, every such schoolmaster to be suitably encouraged and paid by the inhabitants."

Maryland, 1728

Poor Children

"Be it enacted, by the authority, advice, and consent aforesaid, that the master of every public school within this province shall and is hereby required to teach as many poor children gratis, as the visitors, or the major part of them, shall order, or be immediately discharged and removed from his trust in the said school and a new master put in."

Virginia, 1756

Land for Free School

"Whereas, Henry Peasly, formerly of the county of Gloucester, deceased, was in his life-time, and at the time of his death, seized in fee simple of a tract or parcel of land containing six hundred acres, or thereabouts, lying and being in the parish of Abingdon, in the said county, and being so seized, by his last will and testament, in writing, bearing date the seventeenth day of March, in the year of our Lord, one thousand six hundred and seventy-five, devised the same by description of the land he then lived on, together with the ten cows and one breeding mare, for the maintenance of a free school forever, to be kept with a schoolmaster for the education of the children of the parishes of Abingdon and Ware forever.

"And, whereas, several sales have been, by different persons, since the above devise, given for the same purposes, but by reason of the inconvenient situation of said land few children frequent the free school kept there, so that the charitable intention of the said Henry Peasly, and other donors, is of little benefit to the said two parishes.

"And whereas, it is represented to this present General Assembly by the ministers, church wardens and vestrymen of the said two parishes of Abingdon and Ware, that if proper persons were empowered to lease out the said land and slaves, the annual rents thereof would be sufficient to support and maintain a free school in each of the said parishes for the education of children residing there.

"The said trustees and governors shall issue and apply the rents of the said tract or parcel of land, slaves and other premises for the erecting, maintaining and supporting a free school and schoolmaster in each of the said parishes forever, for the education of the children of the said parishes respectively."

New Hampshire, 1771

Bills of Credit

"Whereas, the sum of twenty pounds is set and imposed by an act of this province, passed in the fifth year of the resign of his late majesty, King George the First, as a fine for towns for not keeping a school as therein directed, and the sum of twenty pounds, set and imposed by another act of this province, passed in the seventh year of the same reign, as a fine on selectmen for neglecting to keep a school as therein directed, were originally set in paper bills of credit, no ways adequate to the nominal sum in lawful money at this time.

"And the taking of the nominal sum in lawful money at this time, would be contrary to the original intention of the legislature and injurious to his majesty's subjects; therefore be it enacted by the governor, council and Assembly, that, for the sum of twenty pounds, in each of the acts, aforesaid contained, shall be taken the sum of ten pounds respectively, and no more."

Scolding

olonial lawmakers generally sought to keep women in their place — and that place for the most part was in the home, obedient and silent.

In many instances Colonial laws specifically singled out "scolding wife" in their wording. While it may seem shocking today, it may not be so entirely surprising when considered in light of the fact that even as late as the dawn of the twentieth century chiding or bearing a harsh reproof was ascribed to "one who habitually scolds, especially a rude, clamorous woman," as one popular dictionary states.

Colonial law in other cases, and other locations, did not necessarily single out wives. It sometimes merely noted any person who might be "railing and scolding" in the community. However defined, that person was usually dealt with harshly.

While the ever-present ducking stool could be used for crimes other than scolding, it was particularly adapted for scolding. John Dillon in his nineteenth century volume, *Oddities of Colonial Legislation*, observes that the ducking stool "was ancient engine for the punishment of scolds and delinquent brewers and bakers."

Aside from the ducking stool, those accused and convicted of the act of scolding could sometimes even face a more severe punishment including a public flogging.

"A scolding wife, if reported to a local official, was sentenced to be ducked into water, or to have a cleft stick placed upon her tongue for a portion of the day," relates the grim account by historian Fremont Wirth. "Much of the same punishment was meted out to gossips and disturbers of the peace, though the pillory and the public whipping post were on some occasions used instead."

By the 1670s ,the term for verbally belittling someone in a loud and continuing way, scolding, had been around for more than one hundred years.

Massachusetts, 1672

The Evil Practice

"Whereas, there is no express punishment, by any law hitherto established, affixed to the evil practice of sundry persons by exorbitance of tongue in railing and scolding.

"It is therefore ordered, that all such persons, convicted before any court or magistrate that hath proper cognizance of the case, shall be gagged or set in a ducking-stool, and dipped over head and ears three times in some convenient place of fresh or salt water, as the court or magistrate shall judge."

Slavery

I t would be nearly impossible to truly describe or depict the horrors of human slavery either in the Colonial era or in any other period of time. It is possible, however, to detail some of the incredibly harsh and cruel laws African slaves were forced to endure in the early days of the American Colonies.

The enslavement of Africans existed internationally at least by the 1400s, when regular slave traffic steadily involved many locations throughout Europe, however it was not an immediate part of the Colonial culture.

It is known that white settlers attempted to enslave Native Americans, but as noted in this book's section on Indians, the natives themselves proved to be unsuitable workers in slave conditions. They would eventually be replaced with African slaves.

Ironically some historical accounts indicated the first Africans who landed in the British Colonies during the early years of settlement were not slaves. They were indentured servants, who, like white indentured servants, worked for a period of years to pay for the Atlantic Ocean transportation. Once that contracted debt had been paid, they were able to settle their own land.

In 1619, the first African slaves arrived in the Virginia Colony of Jamestown. They would be the first of thousands of black slaves brought to the New World as merely property.

Early on, however, many of the Colonies were against slavery and even passed various acts opposing its practice on moral grounds. British rulers were not so concerned.

"Among the English, by whom the slave trade had already long been carried on with the West Indies, there were not such scruples," note historians Ernest Bogart and Donald Kemmerer in the volume, *Economic History of The American People*.

From a practical standpoint the economic advantages of slave labor in Colonial America were clear.

For one it was a relatively rapid method of providing much needed labor for tending to Colonial crops and products. Slaves could be deployed into fields by nearby scant living quarters. They had no rights and were paid no wages.

Further, slaves were preferred to indentured servants, for unlike the indentured servants whose contract called for a limited time of service, slaves served for their lifetime. Moreover the children of slaves became the property of the masters and provided still another generation of laborers.

Additionally the cost maintenance for slaves was much less than that of an indentured servant. Slaves received no due or special payments that might have been paid at the end of service to deserving indentured servants.

Until the mid-1600s there were comparatively few African slaves laboring in the field of the Colonies. However, in 1661 the Virginia Assembly enacted laws making slavery legal and soon the number of slaves sold by Dutch slave traders increased greatly.

Again in the 1660s a British Committee on Foreign Plantations declared, "Black slaves are the most useful appurtenances of a plantation." Much later the Lords Commissioners for Trade Plantations further echoed, "the Colonies could not possibly subsist" without an adequate supply of slaves.

In the Virginia Colony money was to be made in growing tobacco; however, it was labor intensive and the obvious solution was found in African slaves. Slaves were consequently brought in large numbers to toil the vast tobacco fields. Meanwhile, in nearby Carolina, planters raised rice on huge tracts of land and found the need for similar slave labor.

"The effect of the introduction of servile labor was to aid the rapid clearing of the land and promote the production of new wealth," according to Bogart and Kemmerer. "Without the system of slavery and the sister institution of white servitude, it may be said that the development of the South could have been much slower and very different in kind."

Then there was the rum trade.

The distillation of rum was an exceptionally profitable business in the New England Colonies. As it happened, a major ingredient of fine rum was the molasses made in the West Indies. The Colonists used the molasses to make rum that was then shipped to Africa where it was traded for slaves.

Accordingly slave ships carried the African slaves to the West Indies where they were sold. The ships then brought barrels of molasses back to the New England Colonies on the third leg of their vicious voyage. Many Colonial merchants became wealthy in the midst of it all. Other Colonials, meanwhile, were busy either distilling the molasses into rum or busy building ships used in continuing the slave trade.

Overall it is difficult to fully know the specific number of African slaves brought from Africa to America and the Colonies during that period. In the *History of Domestic and Foreign Commerce*, author Emory Richard Johnson estimates that during the fifty years preceding the American Revolution the annual importations of black slaves into the continental American Colonies "must have averaged 10,000, and possibly much more than that number."

Wythe House Garden, Williamsburg, Virginia.

Supper Room, Governor's Palace, Williamsburg, Virginia.

The resident slave population, based on slave ships and the natural population increase, steadily increased the number of Africans in the Colonies. It had risen to an estimated 59,000 in 1714. That was a time when advertisements in Colonial newspapers commonly offered "parcels of Negroes" for sale — such "parcels" included men, women, boys, and girls.

By the 1750s there was approximately 300,000 African slaves living in the Colonies. The first federal census in 1790 put the total number of black slaves at very near 700,000.

Carolina, 1669

Christian Slaves

"Since charity obliges us to wish well to the souls of all men, and religion out to alter nothing in any man's civil estate or right, it shall be lawful for slaves, as well as well as others, to enter themselves and be of what church or profession any of them shall thing best, and thereof be as fully members as any freeman.

"But yet no slave shall hereby be exempted from that civil dominion his master hath over him, but be in all things in the same estate and condition he was in before."

Virginia, 1669

Killing Slaves

An act of the casual killing of slaves.

Whereas, the only law in force for the punishment of refractory servants resisting their master, mistress or overseer can not be inflicted upon negroes, nor the obstinacy of many of them by other than violent means suppressed, but it enacted and declared by the General Assembly:

"If any slave resist his master, or other by his master's correcting him, and by the extremity of the correction should chance to die, that his death shall not be accounted felony, but the master or that other person appointed by the master to punish him be acquit from molestation, since it cannot be presumed that prepense malice, which alone makes murder a felony, should induce any man to destroy his own estate."

Virginia, 1680

Slave Insurrections

"Whereas, the frequent meeting of Negro slaves, under pretense of feasts and burials, is judged of dangerous consequence; for prevention whereof for the future, be it enacted by the king's most excellent majesty, by and with the consent of the General Assembly, and it is hereby enacted by the authority aforesaid, that from and after the publication of this law:

"It shall not be lawful for any Negro or other slave to carry or arm himself with any club, staff, gun, sword, or any other weapon of defense or offense, nor to go or depart from off his master's ground without a certificate from his master, mistress or overseer, and such permission not to be granted but upon particular and necessary occasions.

"And every Negro or slave so offending not having a certificate as aforesaid, shall be sent to the next constable, who is hereby enjoined and required to give the said Negro twenty lashes on his bare back, will laid on, and so sent home to his said master, mistress or overseer.

"And it is further enacted by the authority aforesaid, that if any Negro or other salve shall presume to lift up his hand in opposition against any Christian, shall, for every such offense, upon due proof made thereof by oath of the party before a magistrate, have and receive thirty lashes on his bare back, well laid on.

"And it is hereby further enacted by the authority aforesaid, that if any Negro or other slave shall absent himself from his master's service and lie hid and lurking in obscure places, committing injuries to the inhabitants, and shall resist any person or persons that shall, by any lawful authority, be employed to apprehend and taken the said Negro, that then in case of such resistance, it shall be lawful for such person or persons to kill the said Negro or slave so lying out and resisting, and that this law be once every six months published at the respective county courts and parish churches within this colony."

New Jersey, 1682

Selling Without Permission

"And be it enacted, by the authority aforesaid, that all and every person within this province, in case any Negro or Indian slave or servant shall tender, bring or offer to sell, barter or trade with any matter or for anything to any person without permission or license of his master or mistress, such Negro slave or servant shall and may be taken up and whipped by the person or persons to whom he shall tender such sale.

"And such person whipping such Negro or Indian slave or servant shall have the reward of half a crown paid to him by the master or mistress of such Negro or Indian slave or servant."

Carolina, 1687

Ticketing Slaves

"Be it enacted by his Excellency, William, Early of Craven, palatine, and the rest of the true and absolute lords and proprietors of the province, by and with the advice and consent of the commons in this present parliament assembled.

"And it is hereby enacted, by the authority of the same, that no person whatsoever shall send or give leave to any Negro of Indian slave under his or their care, charge or ownership, to go out of their plantations, unless such as usually wait on persons, without a ticket, or one or more white men in their company, in which ticket shall be expressed their names and numbers, and also from and to what place they are intended for, and time, on penalty of forty shillings and paying for taking up such slave as a runaway.

"And whosoever shall not endeavor to apprehend any Negro or Indiana slave, coming into their plantations aforesaid, or where they have care or charge, except such as have tickets before excepted as aforesaid, and apprehending any, shall not punish them by moderate whipping, shall forfeit forty shillings.

"And if any Negro or Indian slave shall offer any violence, by striking or the like, to any white person, he shall, for the first offense, be severely whipped by the constable by order of any justice of the peace; and for the second offense, by like order, shall be severely whipped, his or her nose slit and face burnt in some place.

"And for the third offense to be left to two justices and three sufficient freeholders to inflict death, or any other punishment, according to their discretion: provided such striking or conflict be not by command of, or in lawful defense of, their owner' persons."

Carolina, 1691

Not On The Sabbath

"Be it enacted that any master, mistress or overseer who shall cause or encourage any slave or slaves to work on the Sabbath day, shall forfeit for every offense, for every slave, the sum of five shillings."

Carolina, 1695

Stealing Boats

"If any slave or Indian, at any time after the ratification of this act, shall take away or let loose any boat or canoe or steal any grappling, painter, rope, sail or oars from any landing or place whatsoever, where the owners or persons in whose service and employment they were last in had made fast or laid the same.

"Shall, for the first offense he or they shall be convicted of, receive on his or their bare backs thirty-nine lashes; and for the second offense, shall forfeit and have cut off from his or their heads one ear."

Massachusetts, 1703

Freeing Slaves

"Whereas, great change and inconvenience have arisen to diverse towns and places by the releasing and setting at liberty mulatto and Negro slaves, for the prevention whereof for the future, be it declared and enacted by his Excellency, the governor, council and representatives in general court assembled, and by the authority of the same.

"That no mulatto or Negro slave shall hereafter be manumitted, discharged or set free until sufficient security be given to the treasurer of the town or place where such person dwells, in a valuable sum, not less than fifty pounds, to secure and indemnify the town or place from all charges for or about such mulatto or Negro to be manumitted or set at liberty, in case he or she, by sickness, lameness, or otherwise be rendered incapable to support himself or herself.

"And no mulatto or Negro hereafter manumitted shall be deemed or accounted free for whom security shall not be given as aforesaid; but shall be the proper charge of their respective masters or mistresses, in case they stand in need of relief and support, not withstanding any manumission or instrument of freedom to them made or given.

"And shall also be liable at all times to be put forth to service by the selectmen of the town."

Virginia, 1705

Outlying of Slaves

"Whereas, many times, slaves run away and lie out, hid and lurking in swamps, woods and other obscure places, killing hogs and committing other injuries to the inhabitants of this, her majesty's colony and dominion.

"Be it therefore enacted, and in all such cases, upon intelligence given of any slaves lying out, as aforesaid, any two justices of the peace of the county wherein such slave is supposed to lurk or do mischief, shall be and are empowered and required to issue proclamation against all such slaves, reciting their names, and owners' names, if they are known, and thereby requiring them, and everyone of them, forthwith to surrender themselves.

"And also empowering the sheriff of the said county to take such power with him as he shall think fit and necessary for the effectual apprehending such outlying slave or slaves, and go in search of them.

"Which proclamation shall be published on a Sabbath day, at the door of every church and chapel in said country, by the parish clerk or reader of the church, immediately after divine worship; and in case any slave against whom proclamation hath been thus issued and once published at any church or chapel, as aforesaid, stay out and do not immediately return home, it shall be lawful for any person or persons whatsoever to kill and destroy such ways and means as he, she or they shall think fit, without accusation or impeachment of any crime for the same.

"And if any slave that hath run away and lain out, as aforesaid, shall be apprehended by the sheriff, or any other person, upon the application of the owner of the said slave, it shall and may be lawful for the county court to order such punishment to said slave, either by dismembering or any other way, not touching his life, as they in their discretion shall think fit for the reclaiming any incorrigible slave and terrifying others from the like practices.

"Provided always, and it is further enacted, that for every slave killed, in pursuance of this act, or put to death by law, the master or owner of such slave shall be paid by the public."

New York, 1706

Baptism of Slaves

"Whereas, diverse of her majesty's good subjects, inhabitants of this Colony, now are, and have been willing that such Negro, Indian and mulatto slaves, who belong to them and desire the same should be baptized, but are deterred and hindered there from by reason of a groundless opinion that hath spread itself into this Colony, that by baptizing of such Negro, Indian, or mulatto slave they would become free and ought to be set at liberty.

"In order, therefore, to put an end to all such doubts and scruples as have, or hereafter at any time may arise about the same, but it enacted by the governor, council and assembly, and it is hereby enacted by the authority of the same, that the baptizing of any Negro, Indian, or mulatto slave shall not be any cause or reason for setting them or any of them at liberty."

No Slave Witnesses

"No slave, whatsoever, in this Colony, shall, at any time, be admitted as a witness for or against any freeman, in any case, matter or cause, civil or criminal, whatsoever."

Provincial Council of Pennsylvania, 1707

Punishment for Burglary

In 1707, Philadelphia two slaves, Toney and Quashy, were convicted of the crime of burglary. The court prescribed the death penalty for the two slaves but the slave owners petitioned the Provincial Council of Pennsylvania to spare their lives because their loss would be a "very great" financial hardship.

Instead the slave owners ask in their petition that the slaves be given "corporal punishment as may be requisite for a terror to others of their color."

The Council granted the petition and ordered that the slaves be punished in the following manner:

"They shall be led from the market place, up the second street and down through the front street to the bridge, with their arms extended and tied to a pole across their necks, a cart going before them, and that they shall be severely whipped, all the way as they pass, upon the bare back and shoulders.

"This punishment shall be repeated for three market days successively; in the meantime they shall lie in irons in the prison, at the owners' charge, until they have such an opportunity as shall best please them for transportation: all of which being duly preformed, the sentence of death be entirely remitted."

Carolina, 1722

Pretending Hunger

"Whereas, Negroes and other slaves, under pretense of hunger, do frequently break open corn-houses and rice-houses, and steal from thence corn and rice, and such offenses have been deemed burglary.

"Be it therefore enacted by authority aforesaid, that for the first offense of this kind he shall not suffer death, but be punished with branding on the right cheek and be whipped not exceeding thirty-nine lashes.

"For the second offense, he shall be branded on the left cheek and be whipped not exceeding thirty-nine lashes; and for the third offense, he shall suffer death; anything herein before contained to the contrary notwithstanding."

Killing Slaves

"If any Negro or other slave, under punishment by his master, or his order, for running away or any other crimes or misdemeanors towards his said master, unfortunately shall suffer in life or member, which seldom happens, no person shall be liable to any penalty therefore.

"But if any person shall, out of cruelty, or willfully kill a Negro or other slave of his own, he shall pay into the public treasury fifty pounds proclamation money.

"But if he shall so killed the slave of another man, he shall pay to the owner of the Negro slave the full value, and into the public treasury fifty pounds proclamation money; but not to be liable to any other punishment or forfeiture for the same."

Maryland, 1723

Slaves Striking White Person

"If it shall so happen, at any time, that any Negro or other slave shall strike any white person, it shall and may be lawful, upon proof made thereof, either by the oath of the party so struck or otherwise, before any justice of the peace, for such justice to cause one of the Negro's other slave's ears so offending to be cropped."

Virginia, 1723

Emancipating Slaves

"It be further enacted by the authority aforesaid, that no Negro, mulatto or Indian slaves shall be set free upon any pretense whatsoever, except for some meritorious services, to be adjudged and allowed by the governor and council for the time being, and a license thereupon first had and obtained.

"And that were any slave shall be set free by his master or owner, otherwise than is herein before directed, it shall and may be lawful for the church wardens of the parish wherein such Negro, mulatto or Indian shall reside for the space of one month next after his or her being set free, and they are hereby authorized and required to take up and sell the said Negro, mulatto or Indian as slaves, at the next court held for the said county, by public outcry; and that the moneys arising by such sale shall be applied to the use of the said parish by the vestry thereof."

Maryland, 1729

Punishment For Certain Crimes

"Whereas, several petit treasons and cruel and horrid murders have been lately committed by Negroes, which cruelties they were instigated, and hereafter may be instigated, to commit with the like inhumanity, because they have no sense of shame or apprehension of future rewards or punishments.

"And that the manner of executing offenders prescribed by the laws of England is not sufficient to deter a people from committing the greatest cruelties, who only consider the rigor and severity of punishment.

"Be it therefore enacted by the right honorable the lord proprietary, by and with the advice and consent of his lordship's governor, and the upper and lower houses of Assembly and the authority of the same, that when any Negro or other slave shall be convict by confession or verdict of a jury or any petit treason or murder, or willfully burning of dwelling houses, it shall and may be lawful for the justices before whom such conviction shall be, to give judgment against such Negro or other slave to have the right hand cut off, to be hanged in the usual manner, the head severed from the body, the body divided into four quarters, and head and quarters set up in the most public places of the county where such act was committed."

North Carolina, 1729

Slaves Shall Not Hunt

"Whereas, great damages are frequently done by slaves being permitted to hunt or range with dogs or guns; for prevention whereof, be it enacted by the authority aforesaid, and it shall not be lawful for any slave, on any pretense whatsoever, to go, range or hunt on any person's land other than his master's, with dog or gun, or any weapon, unless there be a white man in his company, under penalty of twenty shillings, to be paid by his master, for every offense, unto the owner of the land whereon such slave shall range or hunt.

"And that no slave shall travel from his master's land by himself to any other place, unless he shall keep the most usual and accustomed road; and if any slave shall offend contrary hereto, it shall be lawful for the owner of the land whereon any slave shall be found, to give him a severe whipping, not exceeding forty lashes.

"And if any loose, disorderly, or suspected person be found drinking, eating, or keeping company with slaves, in the nighttime, such person shall be apprehended and carried before a justice of the peace; and if he can not give a good and satisfactory account of his behavior, such person shall be whipped, at the discretion of the justice, not exceeding forty lashes.

"And for the better suppressing of Negroes traveling and associating themselves together in great numbers, to the terror and damage of the white people, be it enacted by the authority aforesaid, that if any Negro or Negroes shall presume to travel in the night, or be found in the quarters or kitchens among other persons' Negroes, such Negroes so found shall receive correction, not exceeding forty lashes, as aforesaid; and such Negroes in whose company they shall be found shall receive correction, not exceeding twenty lashes.

"Provided always, that nothing in this act shall be construed to prevent any person from sending his slaves on his lawful business, with a pass in writing; nor hinder neighbors' Negroes intermarrying together, so that license being first had and obtained of their several masters."

New York, 1730

Three Slaves Only

"Forasmuch as the number of slaves in the cities of New York and Albany, as also within the several counties, towns and manors within this Colony, doth daily increase, and that they have been oftentimes guilty of confederating together in running away, and other ill and dangerous practices.

"Be it therefore enacted by the aforesaid authority, that it shall not hereafter be lawful for above three slaves to meet together at any time, nor any other place, than when it shall happen they meet in some servile employment for their masters' or mistresses' profit, and by their masters' or mistresses' consent, upon the penalty of being whipped upon the naked back, at the discretion of any one justice of the peace, not exceeding forty lashes for each offense."

Masters Discretion

"Hereafter it shall and may be lawful for any master or mistress to punish his, her or their slave or slaves for their crime and offenses at discretion, not extending to life or limb."

Virginia, 1732

Stealing Slaves

"Whereas, diverse wick and evil disposed persons, intending the run and impoverishing of their fellow subjects, have devised and of late times frequently practiced in several parts of this Colony, unlawful and wicked courses, in secretly taking and carrying away sundry Negro, mulatto and Indian slaves.

"And conveying them out of this dominion or into places remote or unknown to the owners of such slaves, to the insupportable wrong and damage of many of his majesty's good subjects.

"For prevention whereof, be it enacted, by the lieutenant-governor, council and burgesses of this present General Assembly, and it is hereby enacted and declared, by the authority of the same, that if any person or persons, from and after the passing of this act, shall steal any Negro, mulatto or Indian slave, the person or persons so offending shall be declared to be felons, and shall suffer death without benefit of clergy."

South Carolina, 1740

Slave Clothing

"Whereas, many of the salves of this province wear clothes much above the condition of slaves, for procuring whereof they use sinister and evil methods; for the prevention, therefore, of such practices for the future, be it enacted by the authority aforesaid.

"That no owner or proprietor of any slave, Negro or other slave, except livery men and boys, shall permit or suffer such Negro or other slave to have or wear any sort of apparel whatsoever finer, other, or of greater value than Negro cloth, duffels, kerseys, osnabrigs, blue linen, check linen, or coarse garlix or calicoes, checked cottons of Scotch plaids, under the penalty of forfeiting all and every such apparel and garment that any person shall permit or suffer his Negro or other slave to have or wear, finer, other or of greater value than as aforesaid.

"And all and every constable and other persons are hereby authorized, empowered and required, when and as often as they shall find any Negro slave or other slave having on or wearing any sort of garment or apparel whatsoever finer, other or greater value than as aforesaid, to seize and take away the same, to their own use, benefit and behoove, any law, usage or custom to the contrary notwithstanding."

Overworking Slaves

"Whereas, many owners of slaves, and others who have the care, management and overseeing of slaves, do confine them so closely to hard labor that they have not sufficient time for natural rest.

"Be it therefore enacted, by the authority aforesaid, that if any owner of slaves, or other person who shall have the care, management or overseeing of any slaves, shall work or put to labor any such slave or slaves, more than fifteen hours in four and twenty hours, from the twenty-fifth day of March to the twenty-fifth day of September, or more than fourteen hours in four and twenty hours, from the twenty-fifth day of September to the twenty-fifth day of March, every such person shall forfeit any sum not exceeding twenty pounds nor under five pounds, current money, for every time he, she or they shall offend herein, at the discretion of the justice before whom such complaint shall be made."

Penalty For Teaching Slaves to Write

"Whereas, the having of slaves taught to write, or suffering them to be employed in writing, may be attended with great inconveniences, be it therefore enacted, by the authority aforesaid:

"That all and every person and persons, whatsoever, who shall hereafter teach or cause any slave or slaves to be taught to write, or shall use or employ any slave as a scribe in any manner of writing whatsoever, hereafter taught to write, every such person or persons shall, for every such offense, forfeit the sum of one hundred pounds current money."

North Carolina, 1741

Allowance For Killed Slave

"Be it enacted by the authority aforesaid, that if, in the dispersing of any unlawful assemblies of rebel slaves or conspirators, or seizing the arms and ammunition of such as prohibited by this act to keep same.

"Or in apprehending runaways, or in correcting by order of the court, any slave happen to be killed or destroyed, the court of the county where such slave shall be killed, upon application of the owner of such slave, and due proof thereof made, shall put a valuation in proclamation money upon such slave so killed, and certify such valuation to the next session of Assembly, that the said Assembly may made suitable allowance thereupon to the master or owner of such slave."

New York, 1752

No Swearing

"Every Negro, Indian, or other slaves that shall be found guilty of any of the said facts, drunkenness, cursing or swearing, or talk impudently to any Christian, shall suffer so many stripes, at some public place, as the justice of the peace in such place where such offense is committed shall think fit, not exceeding forty."

Spinning and Weaving

Colonialists were given to frequently counting sheep, and not just in their dreams.

Sheep were a vital supply of wool, which was in turn critical to the spinning, and weaving of material suitable for clothing.

One observer wrote of the Colonists in 1643: "They are making linens, fustians, dimities, and look immediately to woolens from their own sheep."

In the 1640s it was estimated that there were more than 3,000 sheep in the Massachusetts Colony alone. Many laws were enacted to protect the sheep and punish anything or anyone that would attempt to harm them.

"The raising of sheep was encouraged in every way," wrote Alice Morse Early long ago in *Home Life in Colonial Days*. "They were permitted to graze on the commons; it was forbidden to send them from the Colony; no sheep under two years old could be killed to sell; if a dog killed a sheep, the dog's owner must hang him and double the cost of the sheep."

Spinning and weaving was viewed with equal seriousness. Women and children who were not earnestly employed in some other meaningful manner were required to spin or weave. Each family was required to provide at least one productive spinner, and spinners were assigned groups that were in turn lead by a group or division director in many of the Colonies.

Moreover, due to the importance of the work, it was assigned to families of all economic levels. The rich as well as the poor were expected to produce the vital fabric. Colonial leaders realized that domestic production was the only solution to complicated and costly importation of textiles from other countries. It was far simpler and financially reasonable to make such material at home.

Thus the homespun industry became a mainstay of Colonial life.

"When the open expression of revolt came, the homespun industries seemed a firm rock for the foundation of liberty," noted Early. "People joined in agreements to eat no lamb or mutton, that thus sheep might be preserved, and to wear no imported woolen cloth."

Laws enforced the thinking. In the Virginia Colony, for example, the Assembly estimated that five children under the age of thirteen could by their (seasonal) work readily spin and weave enough textiles to keep thirty persons clothed.

Colonial spinning and weaving, Williamsburg, Virginia.

Massachusetts, 1672

A Spinning Law

"…Taking into serious consideration the present straits and necessities of the country in respect to clothing, which is not like to be so plentifully supplied from foreign parts as in time past, and not knowing any better way or means conducible to our subsistence that the improving of as many hands as may be in spinning wood, cotton, flax, etc., doth therefore order, and be it ordered by the authority of this Assembly:

"That all hands not necessarily employed on other occasions, as women, girls and boys, shall and hereby are enjoined to spin according to their skills and ability, and that the selectmen in every town do consider the condition and capacity of every family, and accordingly do assess them at one or more spinners.

"And every one thus, aforesaid, for a whole spinner shall, for time to come, spin every year for thirty weeks, three pounds a week of linen, cotton or woolen, and so proportionally for half and quarter spinners, under the penalty of twelve pence a pound short."

Stealing

Stealing was serious business in early Colonial America, with offenders subject to a public whipping, losing an ear, or even being put to death.

As with most crimes of that era one's status in the community might make a difference. Clearly slaves, indentured servants, and orphaned children usually received harsher treatment than others for stealing. In some Colonies the same discrimination applied to women. A woman might be publicly whipped for a particular theft while a man may only be fined for an equal crime.

Those inequities aside, stealing often meant stern punishment. In 1715 Maryland, stealing anything above the value of twelve pence more than once meant branding with a hot iron, "or such other corporal punishment as the court shall judge." The pence or penny was at the time nearly the smallest denomination for a British coin and, in 1736 Massachusetts, the first two convictions for stealing amounted to escalating fines; however the third offense called for the death penalty.

In many of the Colonies stealing someone's pig was a major crime. The first time an offender was caught stealing a neighbor's pig it was usually a heavy fine — perhaps twice the value of the animal. The next time the pig theft might get his or her ears nailed to the frame of the pillory. A third pig theft elevated the stealing crime to a felony and routinely led to the death penalty.

Maryland, 1715

Above Twelve Pence

"If any person or persons have been once convicted of any such thieving and stealing, and shall after been again presented for thieving and stealing of any goods or chattels, laid to be above the value of twelve pence, it shall not be tried and determined by any county court.

"But the party presented, upon such presentment, shall be proceeded against in the provincial court as a felon for simply felony, but shall not be punished by death, but only paying the fourfold, branding with a hot iron, or such other corporal punishment as the court shall adjudge."

Theft By Altering Wills

"In case any person whatsoever shall, at any time hereafter, be legally convicted, by confession or otherwise, of willfully or corruptly embezzling, impairing, raising or altering any will or record within this province, whereby the estate of inheritance or freehold of any person whatsoever shall be defeated, injured, or any ways altered, such person so convicted shall forfeit all his goods and chattels, lands and tenements, the one-half to our sovereign lord the king, his heirs and successors, for the support of government, "And shall also be set in the pillory for the space of two hours, and have both his ears nailed thereto, and cut from off his head."

Massachusetts, 1736

Third Theft Death

"Be it further enacted, by the authority aforesaid, that if any person convicted of a second theft, in manner aforesaid, shall presume a third time to steal any money, goods or chattel, to the value of three pounds lawful money, and be thereof convicted by due course of law, he shall be adjudged to suffer the pains of death without the benefit of clergy."

Highway crime, Colonial painting.

Taverns

averns were the inns of early America and as such they represented a major function in the Colonies.

They not only provided lodging for the weary traveler who came by land or by sea, but hosted those of the community who sought to socialize and communicate. Given the importance of Colonial taverns and the law-driven times, it is not surprising that they were extraordinarily regulated.

Colonial laws not only determined what could be served, but often also the rate it could be consumed. Most taverns could serve beer and some wines. Stronger liquors and even some particular wines generally were not allowed. Other laws also regulated the prices taverns might charge for room and board, and the prices were generally held to modest ranges. Still other laws sometimes mandated that the food and service be of the very best quality.

Further regulated was who could actually own and operate a tavern. Some tradesmen were expressly forbidden from having a license for tavern keeping.

Connecticut, 1650

Regulating Drinking

"Forasmuch as there is a necessary use of Houses of Common Entertainment in every Commonwealth, and of such as retail wine and beer, yet because there are so many abuses of that lawful liberty, both by persons entertaining and persons entertained, there is also need of strict laws and rules to regulate such employment.

"It is therefore ordered by this Court and Authority thereof, that no person or persons licensed for Common Entertainment shall suffer any to be drunken or drink excessively, about half a pint of wine for one person at one time, or to continue tipping above the space of half an hour, or at unreasonable times, or after nine of the clock at night, in or about any of their houses, on penalty of five shillings for every such offense.

"And every person found drunken, so that he be thereby disabled in the use of his understanding, appearing in his speech or gesture, in any of the said houses or elsewhere, shall forfeit ten shillings; and for excessive drinking, three shillings, four pence; and for continuing about half a hour tipping, two shillings and six pence; and for tipping at unreasonable times, or after nine a clock at night, five shillings.

"Provided notwithstanding, such licensed persons may entertain seafaring men or land travelers in the night season when they first come ashore, or from their journey, for their necessary refreshment, or when they prepare for their voyage or journey the next day early, if there be no disorder amongst them.

"And also strangers and other persons in an orderly way may continue in such houses of Common Entertainment during meal times or upon lawful business, what time their occasions shall require."

Raleigh Tavern, Williamsburg, Virginia.

Outside Raleigh Tavern, Williamsburg, Virginia.

Raleigh Tavern, Williamsburg, Virginia

Michie Tavern, Charlottesville, Virginia

South Carolina, 1749

Tradesmen Not Allowed

"Nothing in this act shall extend or be construed to extend to give or grant any power or authority to the said justices, or others, to grant any license to any person or persons who hath or have been bred to or have heretofore used the trade of a carpenter, joiner, bricklayer, plasterer, shipwright, wheelwright, smith, shoemaker, tailor, tanner, cabinet-maker or cooper.

"And shall at the time of his or their application for such order be able and capable, by his or their honest labor and industry, or getting a livelihood and maintaining him or themselves and families by following, using and exercising the trade or trades aforesaid, to which he or they was bred.

"It being the true intent and meaning of this act that no such able tradesman shall, from and after the passing of this act, keep any common tavern, punch house, tippling house or billiard table, or commonly sell wine, cider, beer, brandy, rum, punch, strong drink or other spirituous liquors whatsoever to be spent or consumed in their respective houses."

Thanksgiving

hanksgiving remains a grand and solidly American holiday with a heritage that far predates the official founding of the United States.

With that said, observance of that event has been filled with controversy almost from the beginning. Just when and how it was first celebrated has been open to question. Experts do not even entirely agree on who particularly attended some of the giving of thanks events.

It is known, however, that the observance of Thanksgiving did occur in the Colonies of early America on a somewhat official basis. Here is an example of one such related law.

New Jersey, 1676

Thanksgiving Day

"Whereas, there hast been signal demonstration of God's mercy and favor towards us in this Colony, in preserving and continuing our peace in the midst of wars around us, together with many other mercies which we are sensible of, which call aloud for our acknowledgement and thanksgiving to the Lord.

"Wherefore, be it enacted by this Assembly, that there be a day of public thanksgiving set apart throughout the whole province, to give God the glory and praise thereof, and oblige us to live to his praise and in his fear always, which day shall be the second Wednesday in November next ensuing."

Berkeley Plantation, Site of 1619 Thanksgiving, Williamsburg, Virginia

Tobacco

It is somewhat ironic that one of the greatest cash crops of the American Colonies was often the bane of public consumption.

Modern day smokers and non-smokers may be surprised to know that some rather stringent Colonial laws restricted both the smoking of tobacco by those under age and in most public places.

Tobacco at first was a grand solution for Colonies like Virginia, which sought to be self-supporting. As early as 1612 an ambitious John Rolfe learned the art of curing tobacco, which had long been an agricultural product of Native American Indians. Rolfe was one of the first to make a commercial operation out of tobacco. Further, he fell in love with Pocahontas, the lovely daughter of the great Indian chief Powhatan. He married his bride at Jamestown at an English church in 1614.

"This commodity (tobacco) soon became so valuable a product that it placed the struggling settlement on a better economic basis," wrote historian Fremont Wirth in the book, *The Development of America*. He added, "The hostile attitude of the Indians also changed, at least for a time."

Within a few years esteemed tobacco was given status comparable to money. Ultimately it was considered actual currency in many of the Colonies, and laws specified it as a means of paying fines in criminal cases.

For decades it was the leading item of commerce with England, in part because the demand was so great. Then too with plenty of land and an increasing slave labor population there was almost an unlimited supply of tobacco in the Colonies.

However the economic 'romance' with tobacco did not last forever. By the early 1660s English markets were awash with the Colonial tobacco product. Beyond the oversupply of tobacco, the English themselves were gradually losing their taste for the Colonial-grown crop. Consequently Colonial tobacco prices slumped drastically. All of this led to further regulation of the American tobacco market and enactment of various Colonial laws in the early 1700s.

While all this was transpiring economically, smoking or "the taking of tobacco" was less than acceptable socially in the Colonies.

In many places the use of tobacco was forbidden at the meeting-house or church on Sunday the Sabbath. In some areas smoking tobacco like other offenses relating to the Sabbath, such as labor, was to cease by three on the clock Saturday afternoon.

Moreover, the ruling King James I of England detested the "vile custom of tobacco taking" and publicly condemned it. King James warned in the strongest terms that the "loathsome and hurtful use of this stinking antidote" would soon lead to "corruption and barbarity."

The Colonies also specifically spelled out their objections to tobacco smoking in various sternly worded laws.

Wetherburn's Tavern, Williamsburg, Virginia

Connecticut, 1650

Taking of Tobacco

"Forasmuch as it is observed that many abuses are crept in and committed by frequent taking of Tobacco, it is ordered by the Authority of the Court, that no person under the age of twenty years, nor any other that hat not already accustomed himself to the use there of, shall take any Tobacco, until he hath brought a certificate under the hands of some who are approved for knowledge and skill in the sick, that is useful for him, and also that he hath received a license for the Court for the same.

"And for the regulating of those who either by their former taking it have to have their own apprehensions made it necessary to them, or upon due advice are persuaded to the use there of, it is ordered, that no man within this Colony, after publication hereof, shall take any Tobacco publicly in the street, highways, or any barn yards, or upon training days in any open places, under the penalty of six pence for each offense against this order in any the particulars thereof, to be paid without gain saying upon conviction, by the testimony of one witness that is without just exception, before any Magistrate.

"And the Constables in the several towns are required to make presentment to each particular court of such as they do understand and believe to be transgressors in this order."

Voting

The right to vote was limited in the early American Colonies.

Women could not vote. Slaves obviously could not vote. Servants of any skin color could not vote. People who did not own property could not vote. What democracy remained was left in the hands of white males.

Further qualifications varied from Colony to Colony, but generally the white male voter was required to own a farm or a town lot of significant size. Additionally voters were required to be followers of the Christian faith, and preferably attend within the confines of the established state Church.

There were also stipulations for those who sought to be elected as members of the Assembly. Typically this required the white male person to own five hundred acres of land and own a number of slaves. All totaled the would-be Assembly candidate needed holdings of considerable wealth.

Although some historians have lamented the problem of apathetic voters even in the early Colonial days, the fact is voters were often times mandated to show up and cast their vote. In some cases, failure to vote — if qualified — meant a hefty fine for the offender. Some of the accessed fine, by the way, was then awarded to the person who was observant enough to inform authorities of the offender's misdeeds in not voting as required.

Even qualified voters were sometimes disqualified.

In some regions, if an otherwise eligible voter went afoul of the law and ended up being fined or publicly whipped for "scandalous" behavior, then that voter would be excluded from voting, and perhaps also be excluded from jury duty.

Connecticut, 1650

Not Admitted to Vote

"It is ordered by this Court and decreed, that is any person within these Liberties have been or shall be fined or whipped for any scandalous offense, he shall not be admitted after such time to have any vote in Town or Commonwealth, nor to serve on the Jury until the Court shall manifest their satisfaction."

Maryland, 1716

Voters Required to Appear

"All freeholders, freemen and other persons qualified to give votes in the election of delegates, shall and are hereby obliged to be and appear at the time and place appointed for elections to be hereafter had or made of any delegates, burgesses and citizens to serve in any Assembly for this province.

"Under penalty of one hundred pounds of tobacco for every person so qualified as aforesaid neglecting to appear, one half thereof to the right honorable the lord proprietary, his heirs and successors, for and toward the county charge, and the other half to the informer that shall complain to anyone or more justices or magistrates of such absence; which justice or justices or other magistrates are hereby empowered to determine such complaint and award execution for the said penalty, unless such person or persons shall, at the next county court after such election, show sufficient cause for his or their absence, to be allowed and approved by the justices of the several county courts in this province."

Carolina, 1717

Qualifications of Voters

"Every white man, and no other, professing the Christian religion, who has attained the age of one and twenty years, and hath been a resident and inhabitant of the parish for which he votes for a representative for the space of six months before the date of the writs for the election that he offers to give in his vote.

"And hath a freehold of at least fifty acres of land, or shall be liable to pay taxes to the support of this government for the sum of fifty pounds current money, shall be deemed a person qualified to vote for, and may be capable of electing a representative or representatives to serve as a member or members of the commons house of Assembly for the parish or precinct wherein he actually is a resident."

Virginia, 1769

Penalty for Failure To Vote

"Be it enacted, by the authority aforesaid, that after publication of such writs, and at the day and place of election, every freeholder actually resident within his county shall personally appear and give his vote, upon penalty of forfeiting two hundred pounds of tobacco to any person or persons who will inform or sue for the same, recoverable, with costs, by action of debt or information in the county court of dominion."

Witchcraft

As it turns out it was not the practice of witchcraft that was the evil that spread across the land in early Colonial America. The evil was the persecution of innocent people.

The laws were harsh, the evidence was vague, and the guilt of the accused was predetermined.

Fear and hatred of those believed to be witches had its roots in England and other parts of Europe. Leaders there believed that crafty people who were agents of the devil practiced cunning in the courtroom.

In 1618 ,the book *The Country Justice* was published in London, England. Written by Michael Dalton, it suggested the following for dealing with accused witches before the court:

> "Now against these witches the justices of the peace may not always expect direct evidence, seeing all their works are works of darkness, and not witnesses present with them to accuse them; and therefore for better discovery, I thought good here to insert certain observations of two judges."

The two judges whose observations Dalton valued were Sir James Altham and Sir Edward Bromley. They had published their findings about trying witches a few years earlier in 1612. Their 'pointers' were as follows:

"1. They have ordinarily a familiar or spirit, which appears to them.
2. The said familiar hath some big (swelling) or place upon their body where he sucketh them.
3. They have often pictures of clay or wax, like a man, found in their house.
4. If the dead body bleeds upon the witches touching it.
5. The testimony of the person hurt, upon his death.
6. The examination and confession of the children or servants of the witch.
7. Their own voluntary confession, which exceeds all other evidence."

In studying the laws against witchcraft in the American Colonies, nineteenth century historian John Dillon notes that such were not merely confined to Massachusetts and other New England Colonies. Virginia, Delaware, South Carolina, Pennsylvania, and other English Colonies all adopted similar acts.

In nearly every case, the anti-witch laws mirrored an earlier English act that had been entitled, "An Act Against Conjuration, Witchcraft and Dealing with Wicked and Evil Spirits." It read in part:

"Be it enacted by the authority aforesaid, that if any person or persons shall use, practice or exercise any invocation or conjuration of any evil and wicked spirit, or shall consult, covenant with, entertain, employ, feed or reward any evil and wicked spirit, to or for any intent or purpose.

"Or take up any dead man, woman or child, out of his, her or their grave, or any other place where the dead body resteth, or the skin, bone, or any other part of the dead person, to be employed or used in any manner of witchcraft, sorcery, charm or enchantment; or shall use, practice or exercise any witchcraft, enchantment, charm or sorcery, whereby any person shall be killed, destroyed, wasted, consumed, pined or lamed in his or her body, or any part thereof.

"That then every such offender or offenders, their aides, abettors and counselors, being of any the said offenses duly and lawfully convicted and attained, shall suffer pains of death, as a felon or felons, and shall lose the privilege and benefit of clergy and sanctuary."

Dillon notes that this law remained in effect in Pennsylvania, for example, until September of 1794.

Colonial leaders in the 1600s often took it upon themselves to seek out or search for would-be witches. In 1666, the magistrates appointed for a county in the Colony of Maryland were directed under oath "to inquire, among other things, respecting witchcraft, enchantments, sorceries and magic arts."

In 1674, again in Colonial Maryland, a man named John Connor was convicted and condemned for witchcraft. The Lower House of the General Assembly petitioned for his reprieve, according to Dillon's records. It included a proviso however that the sheriff carry the said Connor "to the gallows, and, the rope being round his neck, it there being made known to him how much he was beholden to the Lower House for their intercession."

A general law enacted within the Colony of New Hampshire in 1680 was a bit more to the point. Under "Witchcraft" was the following act:

"In any Christian, so called, be a witch, yet is, hath or consulted with a familiar spirit, he or they shall be put to death."

The Witch House (1642)

Witch House in 1642, Salem, Massachusetts.

New Jersey, 1668

Perjury & Witchcraft

"If any person or persons shall willingly and maliciously rise up to bear false witness, or purpose to take away a man's life, they shall be put to death.

"If any person found to be a witch, either male or female, they shall be put to death."

Pennsylvania, 1683

Indicted for Witchcraft

Records show that a person named Margaret Matson was indicted for witchcraft late in the year of 1683 in Philadelphia, Pennsylvania. After a charge from the Governor of Pennsylvania, the jury returned with the following curious verdict:

"The prisoner is guilty of the common fame of being a witch, but not guilty as she stands indicted."

Massachusetts, 1692

Witchcraft Hysteria

A majority of sources agree that the Colonial hysteria of discovering so-called witches within the community reached its zenith in the region of Salem Village, Massachusetts. In addition to that part of Salem known as Danvers, it also extended to Essex, Middlesex and Suffolk. Dillon records this account:

"For a time those who were persons of lower classes; but at length some of the first people in rank and character were accused of the crime of witchcraft. The evil had now become awful alarming. Before the close of September in 1692 nineteen persons were excused, and one was pressed to death for refusing to put himself on a trial by jury."

During that witch-hunting year, a Massachusetts Bay Grand Jury returned a bill against one person named Mary Osgood. It read:

"The jurors for our sovereign lord and lady, the king and queen, present, that Mary Osgood, wife of Captain John Osgood, town of Andover aforesaid, wickedly, maliciously and feloniously, a covenant with the Devil did make, and signed the Devil's book, and took the Devil to be her god, and consented to serve and worship him, and was baptized by the Devil, and renounced her former Christian baptism, and promised to be the Devil's, both body and soul forever, and to serve him.

"By which diabolical covenant, by her made with the Devil, she, the said Mary Osgood, is become a detestable witch, against the peace of our sovereign lord and lady, the king and queen, their crown and dignity, and the laws in that case made and provided a true bill."

Interestingly, Mary Osgood was later tried by a jury and found not guilty of being a witch.

In the madness that became generally known as the Salem Witch Hunt more than 150 persons were imprisoned under the charge of practicing witchcraft. Many others were publicly accused of witchcraft but not formally charged. Among those arrested some died before ever being brought to trial. Scores of those where were tried — nearly ever single one — were found guilty. Ultimately nineteen of those accused of witchcraft, including women and five men, were put to death by hanging. None of the condemned was burned at the stake despite a popular misconception that would follow. Accused witches were burned at the stake in European countries like France however.

For the record out of the witch trials at that time, one person who steadfastly refused to enter a plea as to his guilt or innocence was put to death by pressing — a slow painful death involving the gradual adding of heavy stones. The victim, Giles Corey, bravely defined the authority of a tribunal that had clearly put him on trial without sufficient cause.

Virginia, 1692

Innocent or Guilty

Grace Sherwood of Princess Ann County, Virginia was tried for witchcraft after the infamous witch hunt trials of 1692. She came to trial in 1706. According to court records noted by Dillon no decision was rendered despite full consideration of the charges and even court testimony. Apparently the court ordered the sheriff to "take the said Grace into his custody, and to commit her body to the common jail, there to secure her by irons or otherwise, until brought to a future trial."

An irony of the entire witchcraft 'witch hunts' is that in most every case those who freely admitted such crimes escaped punishment. Generally only those who doggedly maintained their innocence suffered severe treatment or death.

Other Crimes and Laws

Colonial law making, order giving, and mandate uttering seemingly had no bounds from the price of bread to provoking language.

Therefore some additional summations from the various Colonies are offered for consideration.

Minutes of Governor and Council of Virginia, 1640

Offending the King

"Stephen Reekes was sentenced to be put in pillory two hours, with a paper on his head expressing his offense, fined fifty pounds sterling, and imprisoned during pleasure, for saying that his majesty was at confession with the Lord of Canterbury."

Massachusetts, 1643

Corn & Bean Election

"It is ordered by this court and the authority thereof, that for the year choosing of assistants the freemen shall use Indian corn and beans, the Indian corn to manifest election, the beans contrary.

"And if any freeman shall put in more than one Indian corn or bean, for the choice or refusal of any public officer, he shall forfeit for every such offense ten pounds, and that any man that is not free, or hath not liberty of voting, putting in any vote, shall forfeit the like sum of ten pounds."

Site of Early Pilgrim Burial Ground

Pilgrim burial ground, Plymouth, Massachusetts.

Virginia, 1655

Gunfire Prohibited

"Whereas, it is much to be doubted that the common enemy, the Indians, if opportunity serve, would suddenly invade this colony, to a total subversion of the same; and whereas, the only means for the discovery of their plots is by alarms, of which no certainty can be had in respect to the frequent shooting of guns in drinking.

"Whereby they proclaim, and as it were, justify that beastly vice, spending much powder in vain that might be reserved against the common enemy.

"Be it therefore enacted, that what person or persons so ever shall, after publication hereof, shoot any guns at drinking, marriages and funerals only excepted, that such person or persons offending shall forfeit one hundred pounds of tobacco, to be levied by distress in case of refusal, and to be disposed of by the militia in ammunition towards a magazine for the county where the offense shall be committed."

Virginia, 1660

Ordinary Sort

"Ordered, that the honorable, the governor, have power to press ten men of the ordinary sort of people, allowing each man two thousand pounds of tobacco per annum for their services, and to employ them toward the building of a state house."

Virginia, 1677

Provoking Language

"Forasmuch as diverse persons do frequently, notwithstanding the late act of Assembly requiring the contrary, renew the breaches, quarrels and heart-burning amongst us in the use by names and terms of distinction: traitors, rebel, rogue, rebel, or such like, by which means it will be impossible ever to unite this colony to its former estate of love and friendship, though wished for and desired by all good people.

"Be it enacted, that whosoever shall presume to use any gravations or terms of distinction aforesaid, and shall be thereof lawfully convicted, shall, for very such offense, forfeit and pay four hundred pounds of tobacco to the use of the parish where such offense be committed.

"And whereas, on the other side, diverse insolent persons, who have been deeply concerned in the late rebellion, will and do notwithstanding their guilt, presuming upon the gracious pardon granted by his majesty, with unseemly, offensive language, urge and provoke those who have been loyal and great sufferers in those late unhappy times to utter in their passion such words as otherwise they would not do, but being highly injurious and prejudicial not only to his majesty's peace, but also to the desired unity of the colony.

"Be it therefore enacted by this present Grand Assembly, and the authority thereof, and it is hereby enacted, that whosoever shall, at any time utter such provoking language to any loyal person whatsoever as shall by the court where the same shall be complained of be adjudged a sufficient provocation for retorting bad language, such person using such provocations be also fined and pay four hundred pounds of tobacco and cask, to be disposed by the vestry to the use of the parish where such offense shall be committed."

Carolina, 1694

Sufficient Fence

"All planters and others of the inhabitants of the province who do plant corn or other provisions, or any other thing which they would have secured from damage or damages or horses, near cattle, or any other stock, shall make, have and keep a good strong and sufficient fence, six feet high, about all sorts of provisions, and shall, from time to time, so maintain and keep the same."

Maryland, 1715

Attorney Fees

"Be it enacted, by the authority, advice and consent aforesaid, that from and after the end of this present session of Assembly, There shall be paid to any attorney or other person practicing the law in any of the county courts of this province, for bringing, prosecuting or defending any action of what nature or quality so ever, to final judgment, agreement or other end thereof, the sum of one hundred pounds of tobacco, unless the principal debt and damage or balance of any debt and damages sued for and recovered do exceed the sum of two thousand pound of tobacco or ten pounds sterling, that then the said attorney shall have two hundred pounds of tobacco and no more.

"And to any attorney or other person practicing the law in the provincial court, high court of chancery, commissary's court, court of vice-admiralty, or for prosecuting or defending any appeals, writs of error or any other matter or thing whatsoever before his Excellency the governor and council, the several sums hereafter expressed and set down, that is to say, for prosecuting or defending any cause, plaint or action of what nature so ever, in the provincial court, to final judgment, agreement or other end thereof, the sum of four hundred pound of tobacco and no more.

"For any fee in the high court of chancery and court of vice-admiralty, six hundred pounds and no more; and to his majesty's attorney-general for any action n in the provincial court, at the suit of his majesty, indictment, presentment of information, the sum of four hundred pounds of tobacco and no more, any law, statue or custom to the contrary in anyway not withstanding.

"And be it further enacted, by the authority, advice and consent aforesaid, that if any attorney or other person practicing law in any of the aforesaid courts do presume to ask, receive, take or demand any greater or larger fee than before by this act appointed, and be thereof legally convicted, he shall be incapable to practice the law in any court of this province for the future."

South Carolina, 1725

Per Head Tax

"Be it enacted and declared by the authority aforesaid, that every hundred acres of land be and is hereby rated at five shillings per hundred acres, and every slave of what age so ever, at twenty shillings per head."

Maryland, 1728

Crows and Squirrels

"Be it enacted by the right honorable the lord proprietary, by and with the advice and consent of his lordship's governor and the upper and lower houses of Assembly, and the authority of the same, that from and after the commencement of this act every master, mistress, owner of a family, or single taxable, in the several and respective counties within this province, shall be and are by this act obliged yearly, to produce to some one of the justices of their county three squirrel scalps or crows' heads for every taxable person they shall pay levy for that year.

"And the justices of the peace before whom such squirrels' scalps or crows' heads shall be brought shall be and is hereby obliged to destroy such squirrels' scalps and crows' heads as shall be so produced to him, to prevent their being produced a second time.

"And give such person a certificate, under his hand, certifying the number of squirrels' scalps and crows' heads such persons brought before him, which certificate the person obtaining the same shall lay before the justices of their county at the time of the laying their county levy; and the justices shall then cause a list of taxable's of their county to be laid before them, in order from thence to compare the number of taxable's each person pays in the county with the certificates produced, that thereby it may be found what persons have complied with this act and who have failed therein."

Virginia, 1732

Attorney's Oath

"You shall do no falsehood, nor consent to any to be done in the court, and if you know of any to be done you shall give notice thereof to the justices of the court, that it may be reformed.

"You shall delay no man for lucre or malice, nor take any unreasonable fees; you shall not wittingly or willingly sue or procure to be sued any false suit, nor give aid nor consent to the same upon pain of being disabled to practice as an attorney forever.

"And furthermore, you shall use yourself in the office of an attorney within the court according to your learning and discretion. So help you God."

South Carolina, 1736

Per Head Tax II

"It is hereby enacted and declared, that the sum of seventeen shillings and six pence, current money, per head, be imposed an levied on all male white persons, from the age of twenty-one to sixty years (except the new-comers settled in his majesty's townships, who are hereby exempted); and the sum of twelve shillings and six pence, current money, per head on all Negroes and other slaves whatsoever and where so ever within the limits of this province; and the sum of seven shillings and six pence, current money, per hundred acres, on all lands throughout the said province (town lots within the limits of Charleston excepted)."

South Carolina, 1744

Tigers, Wolves and Bears

"All and every person and persons whoever that shall hereafter kill in this province, within one hundred and fifty miles of Charleston, or within the Welch tract upon Pedee, any of the beasts of prey hereinafter mentioned, shall have the following rewards.

"That is to say: for a tiger, eight shillings; for a wolf, six shillings; for a bear, four shillings; for a wild cat, four shillings, proclamation money."

North Carolina, 1745

Non-farming Hunters Prohibited

"Forasmuch as there are great numbers of idle and disorderly persons who have no settled habitation nor visible method of supporting themselves by industry or honest calling, many of whom come in from neighboring colonies without proper passes, and kill deer at all seasons of the year, and often leave the carcasses in the woods, and also steal and destroy cattle, and carry away horses, and commit other enormities, to the great prejudice of the inhabitants of this province.

"Be it therefore enacted by the authority aforesaid, that every person who shall hunt and kill deer in the king's waste within this province, and who is not possessed of a settled habitation in the same, shall be obliged to produce a certificate, when required, of his having planted and tended five thousand corn-hills, at five feet distance each hill, the preceding year or season, in the county where he shall hunt, under the hands of at least two justices of the peace of the said county, and the hand of at least one of the church wardens of the parish where such person planted and tended such corn, as aforesaid.

"And be it further enacted, that if any such person as aforesaid is found hunting and does not produce such certificate, as aforesaid, when required, he shall forfeit his gun and five pounds proclamation money for every such offense."

South Carolina, 1749

Preamble to Bread Act

"Whereas, no act of Assembly of this province hath hitherto been made and provided for regulating the price and a size of bread, whereby little or no observance hath been made, either of the due size of reasonable price of bread made for sale within the same, and covetous and evil disposed persons, taking advantage thereof, have, for their own gain and lucre, deceived and oppressed his majesty's subjects, and more especially the poorer sort of people."

New Jersey, 1755

Deerskin Breeches

"Be it enacted by the authority aforesaid, that the commissioners, or any two or them, or any one of them, by the consent of one other, out of the money made current by the act aforesaid, shall purchase for each of the said five hundred men to be raised as aforesaid, one pair of deerskin breeches, which said breeches are allowed to each soldier in lieu of the two pair of osnabrigs trousers ordered to be given to each soldier by the aforesaid act."

Historic Sites

Virginia

Colonial Williamsburg (museums)
PO Box 1776
Williamsburg, VA 23187-1776
757-229-1000
mcottrill@cwf.org

DeWitt Wallace Decorative Arts Museum
(gift shop)
325 W. Francis Street
Williamsburg, VA 23187
757-220-7693

Historic Kenmore House
1201 Washington Ave.
Fredericksburg, VA 22401
540-370-0576

James River Plantations

Berkeley Plantation
Route 5, Charles City, VA
1-888-466-6018
www.berkeleyplantation.com

Shirley Plantation
Route 5, Charles City, VA
1-800-232-1613
www.shirleyplantation.com

Edgewood Plantation
Route 5, Charles City, VA
1-804-829-2962

North Bend Plantation
Route 5, Charles City, VA
1-804-829-5176

Piney Grove Plantation
Route 5, Charles City, VA
1-804-829-2480

Westover Plantation
Route 5, Charles City, VA
804-829-2882

Moore Colonial Farm
6310 Georgetown Pike

Royal Governor's Palace   Williamsburg, Va.

Governor's Place, Williamsburg, Virginia.

KENMORE (BUILT 1752). FREDERICKSBURG. VA.   60575-C

Kenmore House, Fredericksburg, Virginia.

McLean, VA 22101
703-442-7557
http://www.1771.org

Colonial National Historical Park
PO Box 210
Yorktown, VA 23690
757 898-3400

Jamestown & Yorktown Settlement/Victory Center
Williamsburg, VA 23187-1607
888-593-4682
www.historyisfun.org

New Jersey

New Jersey State Museum
PO Box 530
Trenton, NJ 08625
609-292-6464

Morris Museum
6 Normandy Heights Road
Morristown, NJ 07960
973 971-3700
info@morrismuseum.org.

Museum of Early Trades, Crafts
9 Main Street
Madison, NJ
973-377-2982

Old Barracks Museum
Barrack Street
Trenton, NJ 08608
609 396-1776
Barracks@voicenet.com

Allaire Village
PO Box 220
Farmingdale, NJ 07727
732-919-3500

Camden County Historical Society
1900 Park Blvd.
Camden, NJ 08103
856-964-3333
www.cchsnj.com

Massachusetts

Jenny Grist Mill
6 Spring Lane
Plymouth, MA 02360
508-747-4544
info@jennygristmill.org.

Alden House Historic Site
105 Alden Street
Duxbury, MA 02331
781-934-9092
www.alden.org

E-mail addresses of Colonial Sites in Massachusetts

USS Constitution Museum
www.USSconstitutionmuseum.org

Old Manse
www.oldmanse.org

Nichols House Museum
www.nicholshousemuseum.org

House of Seven Gables
www.7gables.org

Salem Witch Museum
www.salemwitchmuseum.com

Salem Heritage Walk
www.thehistrionicacademy.com/salem

Paul Revere House
www.paulreverehouse.org

Old Sturbridge Village
www.osv.org

Old State House Museum
www.bostonhistory.org

Old South Meeting House
www.oldsouthmeetinghouse.org

Concord Museum
www.concordmuseum.org

North Carolina

Catawba Museum of History
PO Box 73
Newton, NC 28658
828 465-0383
cchamuseum@bellsouth.net

Bunker Hill Covered Bridge
PO Box 73
Newton, NC 28658

Historic Murray's Mill
cchjlml@gmail.com

Harper House * Hickory History Center
310 N. Center Street
Hickory, NC 28601
828-324-7294
historicharper@charterinternet.com

The Barker House
505 S. Broad Street
Edenton, NC 27932

Museum of the Albemarle
501 S. Water Street
Elizabeth City, NC 27909
252-335-1453
moa@ncdcr.gov

Newbold-White House
PO Box 103
151 Newbold-White House Road
Hertford, NC 27944
252-426-7567
newboldwhitehouse.com

Somerset Place Historic Site
2572 Lake Shore Road
Creswell, NC 27928
252 797-4560
somerset@ncmail.net

Hope Plantation
132 Hope House Road
Windsor, NC 27983
252-794-3140
hopeplantation@coastalnet.com

Vermont

Historic Windsor
54 Main Street
PO Box 21
Windsor, VT 05089

Maryland

Banneker Historical Park & Museum
300 Oella Street
Catonsville, MD 21228
410-887-1081
mail@friendsofbanneker.org

Dickinson Gorsuch Farm Museum
Van Buren Lane
Cockeysville, MD 21030
410 666-1878

Hampton National Historic Site
535 Hampton Lane
Towson, MD 21286
410 823-1309
hampsuperintendent@nps.gov

Pullen Museum
1824 Frederick Road
Cantonsville, MD 21228-5503
410-744-3034
info@catonsvillehistoroy.org

Historic St. Mary's City
PO Box 39, 18751 Hogaboom Lane
St. Mary's City, MD 20686
240 895-4990
hsmc@smcm.edu

Sotterley Plantation
44300 Sotterley Lane
Hollywood, MD 20636
301 373-2280
officemanager@sotterley.org

St. Clements Island Museum
38370 Point Breeze Road
Colton's Point, MD 20626
302 769-2222
lydiawood@stmarysmd.com

Tudor Hall
41680 Tudor Place
Leonardtown, MD 20650
301 475-2467

South Carolina

Cotton Mill Exchange
301 Gervais Street
Columbia, SC 29201
803 898-4967
cottonmillexchange@museum.org

Charleston Museum
360 Meeting Street
Charleston, SC 29403
843 722-2996
info@charlestonmuseum.org

Old Exchange & Provost Dungeon
122 East Bay Street
Charleston, SC 29401
843 727-2165
youmanst@ci.charleston.sc.us

Georgia

The Midway Museum
PO Box 195
Midway, GA 31320
912 884-5837
info@themidwaymuseum.org

Wormsloe Historical Site
7601 Skidaway Road
Savannah, GA 31406
912-353-3023

Fort Morris Historic Site
2559 Fort Morris Road
Midway, GA 31320
912 884-5999

New York

New Netherland Museum
PO Box 10609
Albany, NY 12201-5609
914-433-9747
info@newnetherland.org

New York State Museum
Rm 3023
Cultural Education Center
Albany, NY 12230
518 449-7860
jguilmet@mail.nysed.gov

New York Historical Society
170 Central Park West
New York, NY 10024
212 873-3400
webmaster@nyhistory.org

Rensselaer County Historical Society
57 Second Street
Troy, NY
218 272-7232
info@rchsonline.org

Museum Village
1010 Route 17M
Monroe, NY 10950
845-782-8248

Historic Richmond Town
441 Clark Avenue
Staten Island, NY 10306
718-351-1611
events@historicrichmondtown.org

Frances Tavern Museum
54 Pearl Street
New York, NY 10004-2429
212-425-1776
www.frauncestavernmuseum.org

Fort Ticonderoga
100 Fort Road, PO Box 390
Ticonderoga, NY 12883
518-585-2821
fort@fort-ticonderoga.org

Federal Hall National Memorial
26 Wall Street
New York, NY 10005
212-825-6990

Pennsylvania

Pennsbury Manor
400 Pennsbury Memorial Road
Morrisville, PA 19067
215 946-0400
willpenn17@aol.com

Heritage Center Museum
5 West King Street
Lancaster, PA 17603
717 299-6440
info@lancasterheritage.com

African American Museum
701 Arch Street
Philadelphia, PA 19106
215 574-0380
info@aampmuseum.org

National Constitution Center
525 Arch Street
Philadelphia, PA 19106
215 409-6600
aberk@constitutioncenter.org

Keith House at Graeme Park
859 County Line Road
Horsham, PA 19044
215-343-0965
ra-graemepark@state.pa.us

Colonial Pennsylvania Plantation
Rock Creek State Park
Media, PA 19063
CPP@netscape.com

New Hampshire

New Hampshire Historical Society
(museum)
6 Eagle Square
Concord, NH 03301
603-228-6688
nhhistory.org

Rhode Island

Museum of Newport History
127 Thames Street
Newport, RI 02840
401-841-8770
www.newporthistorical.org

Roger Williams National Memorial
282 North Main Street
Providence, RI 02903
401-521-7266
www.nps.gov/rowil.index

Delaware

Delaware History Museum
504 Market Street
Wilmington, DE 19801
302-656-0637
www.hsd.org/dhm.htm

Connecticut

Prudence Crandall Museum
Route 169 & Route 14
Canterbury, CT
860-546-7800
crandall.museum@ct.gov

Bibliography

Beard, Charles and Mary Beard. *History of the United States*. New York, New York: The Macmillan Company, 1928.

Bemis, Samuel F. *The Diplomacy of the American Revolution*. Bloomington, Indiana: Indiana University Press, 1965.

Bogart, Ernest and Donald Kemmerer. *Economic History of the American People*. New York, New York: Longmans, Green and Company, 1945.

Curti, Merle and Lewis Todd. *Rise of the American Nation*. New York, New York: Harcourt, Brace & World Inc., 1966.

Dillon, John B. *Oddities of Colonial Legislation in America*. Indianapolis, Indiana: Publisher Robert Douglas, 1879.

Earle, Alice Morse. *Home Life in Colonial Days*. New York, New York: Macmillan Company, 1898.

Keyes, Nelson. *The American Frontier*. Garden City, New York: Hanover House, 1954.

Levin, David. *Cotton Mather—The Young Life of the Lord's Remembrancer 1663-1703*. Cambridge, Massachusetts: Harvard University Press, 1978.

Martin, George. *A Text Book on Civil Government in The United States*. New York, New York: A.S. Barnes and Company, 1875.

Miller, John C. *Origins of the American Revolution*. Boston, Massachusetts: Little, Brown and Company, 1943.

Moore, J. R. H. *Industrial History of the American People*. New York, New York, The Macmillan Company, 1917.

Morris, Richard. *Encyclopedia of American History*. New York, New York: Harper & Brothers, 1953.

Newhouse, Elizabeth editor. *The Story of America. Washington, D.C.*: National Geographic Society, 1984.

Ubbelohde, Carl. *The American Colonies and the British Empire 1607-1763*. New York, New York: Thomas Y. Crowell Company, 1968.

Wade, Richard and Howard Wilder. *A History of the United States*. Boston, Massachusetts: Houghton Mifflin Company, 1968.

Wirth, Fremont. *The Development of America*. Boston, Massachusetts: American Book Company, 1938.